when your child *has...* Dyslexia

✓ Get the Right Diagnosis

✓ Understand Treatment Options

✓ Help Your Child Learn

Abigail Marshall
Series Editor: Vincent Iannelli, MD

adamsmedia
Avon, Massachusetts

Published by
Adams Media, a division of F+W Media, Inc.
57 Littlefield Street, Avon, MA 02322. U.S.A.
www.adamsmedia.com

Contains materials adapted and abridged from *The Everything® Parent's
Guide to Children with Dyslexia* by Abigail Marshall, copyright © 2004
by F+W Publications, Inc., together with new and revised information
about education and treatment options.

ISBN 10: 1-59869-677-7
ISBN 13: 978-1-59869-677-6

Printed in the United States of America.

J I H G F E D C B A

Library of Congress Cataloging-in-Publication Data
is available from the publisher.

*This book is available at quantity discounts for bulk purchases.
For information, please call 1-800-289-0963.*

Contents

Introduction

There is no general consensus on what dyslexia is—how to define it, how to diagnose it, what causes it, or what to do about it. Yet most educators and researchers agree on the symptoms that are commonly associated with dyslexia. You may read five different books that offer five different theories about the cause and best treatment, yet all will list similar sets of traits. In the end, it may be easier to understand dyslexia in terms of what it is *not*—it is *not* a physical disease or illness, it is *not* a problem with your child's eyes or ears, and it is *not* a result of poor schooling or parental neglect.

Dyslexia also is *not* a mental deficiency. Many of the world's most brilliant scientists, creative artists, prominent entrepreneurs, and prolific writers had childhood histories of dyslexia—and many attribute their success to the out-of-the-box thinking style or the inner drive that is part of their learning profile. So dyslexia is best understood as a pattern of strengths and weaknesses which probably arises from normal variations in brain structure and development. Your job as a parent is to encourage and help your child discover and develop her innate talents, while also helping to find ways to overcome areas of weakness.

Keep in mind that reading, writing, and spelling are not natural processes, but rather complex skills that are simply much harder for some children to learn than for others. Your child is a capable learner, but he learns in a different way and on a different timetable than most other children. Even though you can give a name to your child's differences—"dyslexia"—there is no single approach or remedy to the academic problems your child may face. Rather, the information in this book can serve as a guide to help you better understand your child's learning needs and to make more informed choices along the way.

Chapter 1

Understanding Dyslexia

Ten Things You Will Learn in This Chapter

- A working definition of dyslexia.
- How dyslexia may affect your child.
- Genetic influences on dyslexia.
- Some strengths commonly associated with dyslexia.
- Typical areas of weaknesses in learning.
- Some pointers about your child's learning style.
- Right-brained vs. left-brained thinking and dyslexia.
- The connection between dyslexia and the ability to break down the sounds of language.
- Why it is harder for your child to recognize and remember words in print.
- Why your child will learn best with multisensory strategies.

What Is Dyslexia?

Dyslexia is a learning disability that primarily affects your child's ability to learn to read and develop a strong understanding of language. It's more than just a problem with reading; your child may also have difficulties with oral communication, organizational skills, following instructions, and telling time. Sometimes the symptoms can be extremely variable. For example, your child may have problems learning basic math facts and doing arithmetic; on the other hand, he may have a special aptitude for geometry and advanced mathematics. He may be physically clumsy or have poor motor coordination, or he may be especially athletic and talented at sports.

While dyslexia may present certain difficulties to children, it also seems to be associated with many strengths and talents. Your child could be highly imaginative and may excel in art, music, or drama. He might be a good problem-solver, and may be especially good at solving jigsaw puzzles, working with Legos, or playing games of strategy. It's possible that you may have noticed he's handy around the house and has a knack for fixing broken toys and other objects.

DID YOU KNOW?

Dyslexia is far more prevalent than was once believed. In fact, dyslexia may affect one out of five children in the classroom setting. It is estimated that 15 percent of the population has reading difficulties.

What Dyslexia Means for Your Child

Dyslexia is not something that can be outgrown. Over time, your child will gain skills that he struggled with at first, but his dyslexia may present new obstacles as he grows older and school becomes more challenging. He may master reading and writing in elementary school, but have difficulty learning a foreign language in high school. He may avoid early problems with arithmetic, but struggle with algebra. As you learn more about dyslexia, you will be able to anticipate some problems before they arise, and help guide your child to use study methods that are effective and useful for him.

The Biggest Challenge

Reading is the most significant problem area associated with dyslexia. Your child will eventually learn to read, but it will probably take her longer than most other children. It is very common for a child with dyslexia to be unable to read independently until age eight, or ten, or twelve, or even until the teenage years. Despite the delayed start in reading, your child can learn to read advanced material and can gain reading comprehension skills as good as or better than her peers. Having dyslexia, though, means that she'll be more likely to read slowly and with greater effort.

Dyslexia can also affect other areas of life. Your child is likely to have difficulty remembering and following directions and have poor time management skills. She may be tremendously disorganized, or become compulsively neat as a way of compensating for her confusion. These issues can be very frustrating for you and your child, but they are also problems that can be resolved over time with planning and by learning techniques to compensate for weaknesses. For example, as your child grows you will be able to help her become more organized by relying on calendars, planners, and lists; of course, she will need to learn to read first to take advantage of these tools.

A Different Way to Process Information

Dyslexia is caused by differences in how the brain processes information. These differences don't make dyslexia a mental defect or disease, they simply mean that your child has an unusual way of thinking, learning, communicating, and solving problems.

Before the time dyslexia was discovered and labeled, these differences most likely went unnoticed because it was common and acceptable for children to discontinue their education at a young age, grow up to become farmers, artisans, or merchants, or take on other jobs that did not require a formal education. With their strong ability to learn through hands-on practice and apprenticeship, young people with dyslexia probably did quite well.

DID YOU KNOW?

Dyslexia is not caused by poor schools, bad teaching practices, neglectful parenting, or a difficult home life. These factors can explain why many other children also have reading problems, but they cannot cause a child to develop dyslexia.

In today's world, though, strong literacy skills are essential. Increasing importance is placed on school performance and standardized tests; children learn in large classrooms where the "norm" (or average) is fast becoming a minimum standard to which all students are expected to aspire. In this environment, teachers must use the methods that best reach the majority of students in their classrooms. A child with a learning barrier quickly falls behind, and so what was once merely a learning difference has been transformed into a learning disability.

Areas of Cognitive Weakness

Educators and researchers have isolated some factors that seem to play an important role in dyslexia. Most of these are associated with language-processing difficulties or the ability to think sequentially. Mental processing speed also seems to play a part.

The most significant areas of difficulty are:

- Difficulties with phonemic awareness, which is the ability to break down and manipulate the small units of sound in words, such as the three separate sounds for the "c," "a," and "t" in the word "cat."
- Problems with word retrieval or rapid automatic naming, which is the time it takes for a verbal response to a visual stimulus or cue, such as quickly saying the names of letters printed on a chart or names of objects when a picture is shown.

- Poor digit span, which is the ability to store a short sequence of letters or numbers in short-term memory.
- Difficulties with sequencing or concepts of order.
- Visual perceptual confusion, such as the inability to distinguish letters such as "b" and "d," or perceiving letters out of order, such as confusing "was" and "saw," or "from" and "form."

Areas of Mental Strength

Even though dyslexia can cause extreme difficulties with learning, children with dyslexia are usually bright and capable. In fact, dyslexia is not really a single problem or issue, but the name given to a certain common pattern. Individuals with dyslexia tend to be very creative thinkers, with a knack for "out-of-the-box" thinking. Many are artistically talented, and adults with dyslexia usually do well in careers such as engineering, design, or architecture. Recent research shows that children with dyslexia do better on tests of creativity and spatial memory than age-matched children without reading impairments.

Another strength is the intuitive thought process; children with dyslexia often will know the answer to a problem or question, but have difficulty explaining how they arrived at it. This is consistent with a theory that they tend to rely on right-brained, sensory- or image-based thinking rather than language-based mental processes.

Genetic Factors in Dyslexia

Dyslexia is partly inherited, as the tendency to develop dyslexia runs in families. By studying genetic markers in families where there is a high incidence of dyslexia, scientists have now identified genes on at least eight different chromosomes as having some role or connection with dyslexia. No single gene is involved in all cases of dyslexia. It is probable that dyslexia is influenced by a combination of genes; these genes may also influence different aspects of physical or intellectual development. However, because your child's brain continues to grow and develop from birth through adulthood, dyslexia is also influenced by your child's learning experiences and environmental factors. This may explain why the specific symptoms of dyslexia can be so variable, and why some children have much more serious reading problems than others.

Studies of identical twins have shown that where one twin is dyslexic, the other will have dyslexia about 55 to 70 percent of the time, depending on the type of dyslexia. This research shows that there is a strong genetic influence, but that environmental factors also play a part.

Different Styles of Learning

Instead of being viewed as a disability, dyslexia can be seen as the manifestation of a certain learning style. Your child's learning style is the way in which she perceives, conceptualizes, organizes, and recalls information. All children have different areas of strength; good teachers learn to consider these factors in designing their lessons. As you learn more about dyslexia and observe your child, you will also see that you can tie some of the problems she has with a specific pattern of learning. There is no one learning style that all children with dyslexia share, but there are some common patterns that seem to be often associated with dyslexia.

Auditory, Visual, and Kinesthetic Learning

One way to think about learning is to look at it as a process that combines elements of listening (auditory), seeing (visual), and doing (kinesthetic). A child with an auditory learning style will learn best from listening to a lecture or explanation; the visual learner needs to see pictures, graphs, or films to learn; and the kinesthetic learner needs to use his hands or have active participation to learn.

A BETTER PARENTING PRACTICE

A child with dyslexia will learn best with a multisensory approach that simultaneously combines auditory, visual, and tactile learning strategies to teach new facts and concepts. You can help your child learn faster and improve his ability to retain new information by looking for educational approaches that involve seeing, saying, listening, and doing.

Your child's dyslexia may cause conflicts with his dominant learning style. For example, a child with dyslexia often has a predominantly visual learning style.

This works well when he is viewing a film or looking at a picture or diagram. However, it does not serve him when he is being taught to read. The visual learner tends to try to remember words by sight, rather than sounding them out and can often remember information by recalling how it was set out on a page. However, your child's dyslexia will stand in the way of his reading ability. You may be told that your strongly visual child has a poor "visual memory" when in fact his memory for real world objects that he sees is quite remarkable: It is only the memory for letters and printed words that is impaired.

In a school setting, lessons are often geared primarily to students with an auditory learning style. The teacher relies mostly on talking to convey information: he lectures, explains, answers questions. If your child is a visual or kinesthetic learner, she will miss a lot of information; she will simply not be able to learn without strategies that reach her strongest learning modes. On the other hand, if your child has dyslexia but is an auditory learner, her strengths may mask her dyslexia. She may do well in school, relying on her superior listening skills to keep up in class and to learn what is in books by listening to others read aloud. Her dyslexia may go undetected until the later grades, when she will be expected to learn more from independent reading.

Left-Brained vs. Right-Brained
Some people break down two main styles of learning as being left-brained or right-brained. Researchers know that many functions related to language use and

reading are typically localized in the left hemisphere of the brain. The right hemisphere is associated more with intuitive thought and creativity. Of course, the two sides of the brain are designed to work together, and most people develop the ability to use both sides, depending on the task or activity they are engaged in.

Psychologist Linda Silverman, who has worked extensively with gifted children, describes these two styles of learning as being auditory-sequential and visual-spatial. The auditory-sequential learner thinks primarily in words, learns step by step, attends well to detail, learns phonics easily, and excels at rote memory. The visual-spatial learner thinks primarily with images, learns concepts all at once, sees the big picture, learns best by seeing relationships, and learns complex concepts easily but struggles with basic skills.

One possible explanation for dyslexia is that some children who are right-brained learners find it much easier to think about new information and solve problems using their visual-spatial strategies. Over time, they reinforce their own tendencies toward relying on imagery and intuitive thought processes, and fail to develop strong brain pathways for thinking with the sounds of language. Thus, when it comes time for these children to learn to read, their brains simply aren't ready.

Brain Research and Dyslexia

Within the past two decades, scientists have been able to use sophisticated equipment to study the workings of the human brain. With this equipment, scientists can measure electrical impulses, chemical changes, or blood flow through the brain while their research subjects perform specific tasks. This has allowed scientists to look at the mental changes associated with learning to read, and to compare the mental activity of people with dyslexia with that of people who have no reading problems.

Research shows that each brain is different; not all people with dyslexia process information exactly the same way. However, by studying many individuals, it is possible to generalize and to explore common elements that may contribute to dyslexia.

DID YOU KNOW?

Learning new skills can alter brain structure. Researchers recently found that certain areas of the brain grew larger when they taught their subjects to juggle. When the jugglers stopped practicing and their brains were measured again, the brain expansion they had seen earlier was reduced.

Searching for Answers

Good scientific research is limited in scope; scientists are careful to study only one particular theory or question, under controlled conditions. The brain is an extremely complex system, and each research project sheds light on only a small part of the mental processes of learning, reading, and dyslexia. Thus research cannot yet provide all the answers. Instead, each new study provides an intriguing look into another piece of the puzzle. Scientists measure many different responses in children with dyslexia, such as the timing of the brain's response to external stimuli, the way that the brain recognizes letter patterns, and the pattern of activity in the two brain hemispheres associated with different reading tasks.

Response Time and Filtering Information

Scientists have discovered that the brains of children with dyslexia take a fraction of a second longer to respond to certain stimuli than the brains of children who read well; this pattern persists through adulthood. The delayed response time is seen both in tests of listening to the sounds of language and responding to visually presented symbols. These delays could explain why individuals with dyslexia tend to read more slowly.

It is also possible that because of the problem with timing, children with dyslexia may not hear the sounds and rhythms of language in the same way that others do. This may explain why they have difficulty breaking down words into component sounds or blending sounds into words.

Other researchers have found that people with dyslexia have more difficulty filtering out environmental distractions and focusing attention on significant information. This may make it more difficult for them to learn how to form mental categories to distinguish important from irrelevant sensory input—for example, to sort out letters from other marks on a page, or to recognize which sounds of language are significant.

Visual Word Form Recognition

Researchers have also discovered that the part of the brain used to quickly recognize letters, letter sequences, and words in most people does not seem to activate in the brains of adults and older children with dyslexia. In most people, an area in the left visual cortex activates almost immediately upon seeing any sequence of letters; the activity is very brief, and ends within about half a second after the word or letter sequence is first seen. Scientists call this part of the brain the "visual word form area."

DID YOU KNOW?

Skilled readers recognize most words by sight even before becoming consciously aware of looking at a word. This is why silent reading is faster than oral reading. Sounding-out and speaking words is a slower mental process, and requires involvement of brain areas involved in speech production.

People with dyslexia simply do not seem to engage this area when presented with words or letter patterns. Part of the problem may be timing; in most readers, the visual word form area activation is completed in the fraction of a second before the brain begins to activate in research subjects with dyslexia.

The visual word form area may function as an important sorting mechanism, where the brain quickly responds to familiar words and directs unfamiliar words to other left hemispheric areas for further processing.

An inability to use this brain area may explain why children with dyslexia have difficulty with remembering and recognizing familiar words.

Looking into Right Brain Activity

Scientists studying the process of learning to read in typical children have observed that the brain changes as reading proficiency is gained. Very young children have high levels of activity in both the right and left brain hemispheres when looking at letters and words. As children gain the ability to recognize familiar words and letter patterns on sight, the right brain activity subsides, and a strong pattern of left hemispheric activity is observed.

The left hemisphere is important to reading because it contains pathways and regions which are specialized for attending to and understanding the sounds of language. This is the part of the brain that will become specialized for connecting letters to the sounds they represent, and for connecting and blending the individual sounds in a series of letters to form a word.

Other studies have shown that adults and children with dyslexia have more right brain and frontal brain activity than good readers with certain reading tasks. For most people, the left brain hemisphere is also slightly larger than the right. Several studies show that adults with dyslexia tend to have more evenly structured, symmetrical brains, with the right hemisphere being about the same size as the left, and activity less differentiated between left and right hemispheres.

The child or adult who is using right brain processes to try to decipher text is probably getting mixed signals, and will understandably find reading to be a difficult and confusing task. On the other hand, the evidence from these studies helps to explain why the reading problems associated with dyslexia tend to go hand-in-hand with creativity, artistic ability, and strong spatial reasoning skills, as these are abilities associated with the right hemisphere.

How Brain Activity Influences Reading Skills

When scientists study brain activity of children and adults with reading difficulties, they do not know whether the differences they see reflect a structural difference in the brain, or whether they are seeing functional patterns that could be changed with teaching or learning. Since studies show that poor readers do not seem to use the left brain areas for phonetic processing in the same way as good readers, scientists are interested in learning whether specific types of teaching or training can change brain use patterns.

Recent Studies Show Interesting Results

Recent studies show that children and adults with dyslexia can experience changes in patterns in brain activity after receiving training for specific reading skills. For example, when children receive training to increase their sensitivity to phonetics, their brain activity begins to look more like the brains of ordinary readers, at least when performing tasks such as identifying rhyming patterns in listening to or reading words. However, it is not clear whether such changes in brain activity actually promote overall improved reading skills, or carry over to contexts other than the specific tasks that have been studied.

Also, some studies have shown paradoxical results: sometimes the research subjects with dyslexia who are the best readers also show the greatest differences from the norm in brain activity. For example, one researcher, Dr. Sally Shaywitz, looked at the brains of young adults whose progress had been followed from kindergarten and whose dyslexia had been identified by their poor performance in reading skills in early childhood. Some of these young people had grown up to become capable readers, while others remained very poor readers. Surprisingly, the improved readers had a very different pattern of brain use, while the poor readers had brain patterns more closely resembling those of typical readers without dyslexia. When doing reading tasks involving making judgments about word meaning, these improved readers appeared to completely bypass the left hemispheric region used for phonetic decoding, relying mostly on right brain and frontal activity in both hemispheres.

In another study, scientists with the National Institute of Mental Health used tests measuring blood flow in the brain to correlate brain use patterns with reading ability in young adults with and without dyslexia. After testing their subjects for reading ability with common skills tests, brain activity was measured while the subjects were reading sentences aloud. The researchers found that there was an inverse relationship of brain use, dyslexia, and reading ability. Among the group with dyslexia, increased right brain activity correlated directly with improved reading ability. This was the opposite pattern from the group without dyslexia, whose reading ability correlated with increased left hemispheric activity.

These studies suggest that it may be most efficient for a person with dyslexia to learn to use different brain pathways when reading, perhaps because innate differences in brain structure makes it harder to use the left hemispheric pathways typically associated with good reading.

Phonological Training for Your Child

People with dyslexia tend to have difficulty applying and using phonetic rules to decode words. As noted earlier, brain scans show that subjects with dyslexia have reduced activity in the left brain areas normally associated with reading, and increased activity in right brain regions.

Using brain scans conducted before and after intensive, short-term training to improve phonetic skills, researchers have indeed observed that children and adults with dyslexia show increased levels of left brain activity after receiving such training. However, the brain scans have shown that such training also results in higher activation of a number of regions not normally involved in phonological processing, and not typically activated for ordinary readers. These regions include parts of the right side of the brain that are mirror images of the typical left-sided language processing areas. These are brain areas that are associated with image-based thinking, intuitive thought processes, and problem-solving skills.

So, the research seems to suggest that while training can help children and adults with dyslexia use left-brain word-processing areas more effectively, the person with dyslexia is still predominantly a right-brained thinker. While most children can become good readers by learning to rely mostly on left-brain thinking processes, a child with dyslexia will need to learn to harness his natural right-brain mental strengths to build reading skills.

A BETTER PARENTING PRACTICE

The more your child knows about a word, the more likely he is to recognize it in print. Even if your child struggles to decipher text on a page, you can help lay the foundation for better reading by encouraging him to develop a stronger vocabulary and understanding of the meanings of words.

This research may explain why it takes longer for children with dyslexia to learn to read; the process of developing and coordinating right brain thinking with the skill set needed for reading may be more complex and take many years to develop. This research also helps explain why children with dyslexia always learn best with multisensory strategies—approaches that integrate auditory, visual, and kinesthetic learning tools, and thus probably activate more brain regions simultaneously.

Brain Research—What It Really Means

As a parent, you should keep in mind that scientists still have much to learn. Each brain is unique, and even studies that report generalized findings may include some subjects with dyslexia whose brain activity did not fit the pattern that is described. Gender differences can play a part: studies also show that many girls use their brains differently for some tasks than boys. Many of the studies of brain structure and function in dyslexia have looked at only boys and men; the findings may not apply to your daughter with dyslexia.

In any case, your child is not a research subject, but a unique person whose style of thinking and learning is as individualized as her facial features or her finger-prints. Brain research is useful because it helps to under-stand why some children struggle with tasks that seem easy for others, and it helps educators to develop more effective methods of instruction. The most important finding of brain research is simply the knowledge that there may be many different ways to learn; your child with dyslexia will need to discover her own best path to learning over the years as she grows to adulthood.

Chapter 2

Recognizing Dyslexia in Your Child

Ten Things You Will Learn in This Chapter

- Early signs of dyslexia in young children.
- Typical areas of reading difficulty.
- Problems with speech or hearing.
- Issues with vision that may affect reading.
- Common problems for school-age children.
- Some behavior problems associated with dyslexia.
- Typical problems with math and numbers.
- Some common social and emotional problems.
- Some strategies to ease tensions at home.
- About dyslexia in teenagers.

Early Signs of Dyslexia

The symptoms of dyslexia are extremely variable. In fact, your child's symptoms may not even be consistent from day to day. This may lead to the mistaken impression that your child is careless or is simply not trying hard enough. At home and at play, your child might be very adept, but at school she might struggle to master the most basic material.

Because dyslexia is primarily associated with difficulty in learning to read, it cannot be reliably diagnosed until your child is the age at which reading typically begins. Although most children are ready to begin to read at about age six, individual development is also variable. It is normal for some children to pick up basic reading skills as early as age four, and it is also typical for many children to be delayed in learning to read until age seven or eight.

Symptoms of Dyslexia—and How to See Them

Identifying signs of dyslexia can be a difficult task. Many of the problems that are tell-tale symptoms of dyslexia in older children are part of normal development in a three-year-old child. In order to assess whether your very young child could have dyslexia, it's best to look at her overall learning pattern. The following are some common characteristics that may be signs of dyslexia in very young children:

- Jumbling sounds of words in speech, such as saying "pasgetti" for "spaghetti" or "mawnlower" for "lawnmower."

- Confusing words signifying direction in space or time, such as "up" and "down," "in" and "out," "yesterday" and "tomorrow."
- Forgetting or confusing the word for known objects, such as "table" or "chair."
- Delayed speech development.
- Unusual speech patterns, such as frequent hesitations or stammering.
- Difficulty with behavior or learning.
- Difficulty remembering and following directions.
- Extremely low tolerance for frustration.
- Difficulty getting dressed, buttoning clothes, and putting shoes on the correct feet.
- Excessive tripping, bumping into things, and falling over.
- Difficulty with catching, kicking, or throwing a ball; with hopping and/or skipping.

DID YOU KNOW?

Studies show that if a child has a parent or older sibling with dyslexia, there is a 40 percent chance that he will also have difficulty in learning to read. If dyslexia seems to run in your family, you will want to be alert to possible symptoms before your child begins school.

Reading and Writing

If you've noticed that your child has difficulty learning to form letters or frequently reverses letters, it's understandable why there's cause for concern. However, many small children do not have the small motor coordination needed for writing, and reversals of some letters in writing is common in many children up until age seven. Reversals of entire words—"mirror" writing—are less common, but they are not significant in isolation; they are only a sign of dyslexia if accompanied by other symptoms. Although most children will learn to recognize some letters of the alphabet in early childhood, many children are unable to learn to recite or write the letters of the complete alphabet until they reach school age.

Here are some problems with prereading skills that may be early signs of dyslexia:

- Difficulty learning nursery rhymes and rhyming words.
- Difficulty in learning (and remembering) names of letters.
- Enjoys being read to but shows no interest in letters or words.
- Difficulty with clapping a simple rhythm.

Keep in mind that it is important to look at the overall pattern of learning, including strengths as well as weaknesses. Many children simply are not ready to read until they are somewhat older than average; that does not mean they have dyslexia.

Speech and Language

A child who shows significant language delays or difficulties with speech can and should be evaluated by a speech and language therapist. If you or your child's pediatrician suspect a possible hearing problem, you should also seek evaluation from an audiologist. These language problems can be an early sign of dyslexia; they can also indicate hearing or auditory learning problems. If a child is merely late to begin talking, perhaps not speaking or only saying a few words until age three or later, consider how he responds to language. If your child seems to understand what you are saying to him, and responds appropriately to simple instructions, his delayed speech may just be part of his normal developmental pattern.

DOES THIS SOUND LIKE YOUR CHILD?

Delayed speech does not always indicate a learning problem. Research has shown that many highly intelligent children do not start talking until age three or four. Many of these children's parents are musicians or mathematicians; these children usually grow up to have similar aptitudes.

Expression and Articulation

You should be more concerned if your child has continued speech difficulties once he begins talking. Children with dyslexia or other language problems often have difficulty expressing themselves or with understanding what is said to them. Your child may have difficulties with articulation, which is the ability to pronounce specific words correctly. While all young children mispronounce difficult words at first, a child with dyslexia is particularly prone to making errors which confuse the order or sequence of sounds in a word or phrase.

Problematic Speech Patterns

Your child may stutter, hesitate, or stammer. This is called dysfluency, an interruption in the rhythm of speech. Some children have difficulties with voice tones, pitch, and volume. An odd or halting manner of speech can also be an early sign of dyslexia.

Your child may show signs of word retrieval problems. He may often hesitate or be unable to remember the word for common objects, or mistakenly substitute the wrong word, saying one thing when he means something else. He may frequently confuse words related to direction or time; for example, mixing up words like "over" and "under," or "yesterday" and "tomorrow." This word confusion may be apparent in his receptive language as well as his expressive language; that is, he may be easily confused by directions or statements that others make to him using these words.

Your child also may seem to have difficulty learning correct grammar and syntax, such as the use of pronouns. She may have a hard time learning the difference between "he" and "she," or difficulty learning to use "I" rather than "me" when beginning a sentence. All of these problems are very normal at early stages of development, but most children show steady progress and outgrow them over time.

Persistent problems can indicate that your child has difficulty understanding and processing language. These early oral language problems can indicate that your child has difficulty thinking with and understanding the meaning of words. Even though she may outgrow the speech problems, the underlying language issues may remain, giving rise to problems recognizing and understanding words in print.

Your Child's Hearing

Even if your child is speaking and understanding language well, you should be alert to other signs of any difficulties with hearing. Undetected hearing problems can affect the way that your child's sensitivity to the sounds of language develops. Many children with dyslexia suffer from allergies or frequent ear infections in early childhood. Ear infections can cause impaired hearing or intermittent hearing loss, and these may be a contributing factor to development. It is important to seek prompt medical treatment for ear infections and other respiratory illnesses.

DID YOU KNOW?

The National Information Center for Children and Youth with Disabilities estimates that one in ten individuals are affected by a communication disorder. In other words, at least one million children are placed in special education programs as a result of having a language or speech disorder.

Extreme sensitivity to loud noises or sounds with very high or low frequencies (such as the buzz emanated by fluorescent lights or the hum of a fan) may also indicate a problem with the way that your child hears the world around her. If you suspect a hearing problem, you can begin by consulting with your child's physician. He can examine your child and refer you to a specialist if necessary.

Your Child's Vision

Dyslexia is not caused by vision problems, but good vision is important to reading development. One in five preschool-aged children has a vision disorder. Many common vision problems are preventable if detected in early childhood. According to the College of Optometrists in Vision Development, problems in any of the following areas can have a significant impact on learning:

- Eye tracking skills (eyes staying on target, i.e., following a line of print)
- Eye teaming skills (two eyes working together as a synchronized team)
- Binocular vision (simultaneously blending the images from both eyes into one image)
- Accommodation (eye focusing)
- Visual-motor integration (i.e., eye-hand coordination, sports vision, etc.)
- Visual perception (visual memory, visual form perception, visualization, directionality)

Your child can be evaluated for possible vision problems well before she reaches the age when she begins school. As a parent, you should suspect a vision issue if you observe any of the following symptoms:

- One eye drifts or aims in a different direction than the other.
- Your child tilts or turns her head to see.
- Your child's head is frequently tilted to one side or one shoulder is noticeably higher.
- Your child squints or closes or covers one eye.
- Your child seems to have a short attention span for her age.
- Your child has poor hand-eye coordination for activities like playing with a ball.
- Your child avoids coloring, working with puzzles, and other detailed activities.

It is a good idea to arrange a thorough optometric examination for your child by age three to determine whether his vision is developing normally, whether or not you suspect a specific problem. If you are concerned about your child's vision development, it is best to arrange an appointment with a board-certified developmental optometrist who specializes in evaluating and correcting these types of vision problems.

Dyslexia in School-Age Children

In most cases, you will probably not be aware that your child has dyslexia until he is in first or second grade. At that time, when reading instruction begins in earnest, your child is likely to lag behind and to begin to show signs of frustration at school. After several months you may realize that your child simply hasn't caught on to reading in the same way as his peers. He may still have difficulty recognizing letters of the alphabet, or he may know the letters and their sounds but seem unable to put them together to form even simple words. You may notice that he seems unable to remember words that he has seen before, and struggles to sound out every word he sees.

A BETTER PARENTING PRACTICE

Do not wait for the teacher to tell you she suspects a problem before seeking help. Many teachers have not been trained to recognize dyslexia, and they may not recognize the signs in a child who is bright and actively participates in many class activities which do not involve reading or writing.

Symptoms in Children Age 5–12

Not all reading problems stem from dyslexia. In fact, the vast majority of children identified by school authorities as having reading problems are struggling for other reasons, such as socioeconomic factors, language barriers, inadequate preparation for school, or generalized cognitive impairments. Because so many school children struggle with reading for reasons other than dyslexia, your child's teacher may not suspect dyslexia in your child, even if clear signs are there. Unfortunately, most schools do not screen for dyslexia, and very often children are not identified until they have fallen far behind their peers. Thus, it is your responsibility to be alert to possible signs and symptoms.

Problems with Reading and Writing

The surest sign of dyslexia is simply the fact that your child seems bright and capable at home and at play, yet he struggles with reading, writing, and spelling. School-aged children with dyslexia will exhibit many of the following symptoms:

- Confusing letters with similar appearances, such as "b" and "d," or "e" and "c."
- Writing that contains frequent reversals, transpositions, or inversions.
- Difficulty remembering common sight words, even after repeated practice.
- Stumbling, hesitating, or making mistakes or omissions when reading small, easy words like "and" or "from."
- Spelling phonetically and inconsistently (e.g., "foniks" for "phonics").
- Complaining that letters and words on the page move or become blurred.
- Complaining of dizziness, headaches, or stomachaches while reading.

Even when she gains the ability to decode and recognize words and sentences, your child may read and reread material with little comprehension. As she matures and reading demands increase, new problems may arise.

Dyslexia and Math

In addition to problems with reading, your child may experience problems with math. Even if his math skills are strong, your child is likely to have poor rote memory and difficulty memorizing math facts such as multiplication tables. He may be able to do simple arithmetic, such as addition or subtraction, but have difficulty applying or using math concepts when confronted with story problems. Even if your child seems to be good with math, he may often be unable to explain how he arrived at the correct answer or to write out the steps of the problem. All of these issues reflect an underlying problem with language; your child simply has difficulty understanding or remembering math concepts expressed in words.

Transposing numbers or making frequent errors with math symbols could be a problem for your child, such as confusing + and − signs, when copying from the board or textbook. This may reflect a perceptual problem, or stem from the confusion over symbols that is part of dyslexia. Understanding time and time concepts might also be a problem.

Common Behavior Problems

Your first indication that something is wrong may be complaints from your child's teacher about her behavior or problems she is experiencing at school. Some behavior issues may stem from the dyslexia itself; your child's teacher may complain that she doesn't pay attention or follow instructions, or that she is slow to complete class work. These issues may be the direct result of your child's confusion and inability to understand much of what is going on around her.

DOES THIS SOUND LIKE YOUR CHILD?

Sometimes a bright child is able to overcome or avoid issues with reading but will still have an array of related symptoms. The child may have a strong visual memory that allows her to develop good sight reading skills despite having characteristic difficulty with phonetics. The dyslexia may become apparent because of problems with spelling or difficulties with handwriting or written composition.

Other behavior problems may be deliberate and could be an expression of frustration and anger. Your child may intentionally try to disrupt the class to create distractions so as to avoid having to complete assigned work. She would rather that her classmates think of her as funny or bad than stupid. She may even want to incur punishment, if punishment means being sent to sit in the hallway or principal's office. To a child with dyslexia, such punishment can be a welcome reprieve from the torture of the classroom.

Some common behavior problems that your child's teacher may report are:

- Laziness, carelessness, or immaturity
- Daydreaming
- Disruptive behavior
- Being easily distracted
- Resistance to following directions
- Reluctance to work on assignments

To the teacher, all of these behaviors may seem deliberate. However, your child simply does not have the ability to conform to the expectations of a classroom when she is confused or unable to perform work at the same level and speed as the other children. You will not be able to help resolve the behavioral problem unless the learning problem is first addressed.

Social and Emotional Problems

Your child's school problems will probably also be reflected in problems at home and in interactions with his peers. Some of these issues may be directly related to his dyslexia, but many of these issues stem indirectly from the stress and frustration that is a constant part of your child's day.

From the age of seven, if not sooner, your child might be aware of her peer performance in comparison to other children her age. Struggling to understand concepts that other children find easy and making mistakes in schoolwork can be embarrassing. Showing your support and encouragement will help, but these problems will take their toll. Your child might complain of stomachaches or headaches in the morning; while it may seem like an attempt to avoid school, the pain could be a very real manifestation of the stress and anxiety.

A BETTER PARENTING PRACTICE

You can help your child deal with anger and frustration—and help yourself—by teaching him relaxation and stress-reducing techniques, and practicing them yourself. This not only will relieve tension at home, but will also help your child develop greater self-control and improve his ability to focus on his work.

It's easy to become short-tempered and frustrated at times, as dealing with your child may seem to require endless and fruitless repetition, day after day. It's tempting to shout, nag, and make dire threats of punishment. All of this, of course, will only make matters worse, as it will allow your child's dyslexia to become the focus of your home and family life. Confronting these problems will take patience, understanding, and effort on your part. If you can lay aside your own feelings of frustration and disappointment, you'll be able to provide your child with the support and guidance he needs. Try to encourage him to participate in activities he can succeed at, because his self-esteem will be crucial to his development and to peace in your household. Be prepared to set limits; your child needs understanding, but he also needs structure and support in learning to control his own behavior.

Dyslexia in Adolescents

As your child approaches the teenage years, dyslexia can present new challenges. In middle school and high school the academic demands increase tremendously. Additionally, your child will be faced with juggling a number of classes with different teachers, each with their own expectations as to homework and class behavior. Your child may need your help and support more than ever. However, your child is also feeling a natural pull toward independence. When he has academic problems, he may feel embarrassed by your attempts to confer with teachers and prefer to tough it out on his own rather than have his parents act as intermediaries.

Changes and New Challenges

As your child reaches adolescence, he may continue to have the same problems and symptoms that indicated dyslexia in his elementary school years. If a diagnosis has been made and he receives appropriate accommodations and services, you may notice some improvements. Often, after years of struggling and unsuccessful interventions, things seem to suddenly click at around age twelve. This can be a result of normal growth and development. Children at this age are developing a greater capacity for abstract and complex thought, and this very capacity may be the breakthrough your child needed in order to finally put all the elements needed for reading together.

A BETTER PARENTING PRACTICE

Educator Richard Lavoie has made several videos that are helpful in understanding your child's feelings and addressing his negative behavior, including one offering practical advice and showing how preventive discipline can anticipate many problems before they start. You can find them at *www.ricklavoie.com*.

Additionally, changed expectations at school may benefit your child. With separate teachers for most of his classes, he may finally have the opportunity to excel in his areas of strength. It will become more common for written homework to be completed with a computer and word processor, and your child may become adept at using the computer spell checker and grammar checker in completing his work. As math courses become more demanding, the use of the calculator becomes routine and expected. Your child may be able to round out his day with elective courses in art or music, and may find his niche in athletic or other extracurricular activities.

On the other hand, if your child's needs have not been met in the past, the social and behavioral problems that result from her frustration and low self-esteem may be magnified. As a way of dealing with their problems, teenagers may sometimes cut class or skip school, provoke conflict with teachers and administrators at school, or experiment with illicit drugs and alcohol, sexually promiscuous behavior, or engage in criminal acts such as shoplifting. Sometimes children show signs of serious depression or suicidal thoughts when they don't know how to handle their frustration.

These social and behavioral problems are not a direct result of dyslexia; many children who have never had school problems in the past will also rebel and break rules in their high school years. However, a child who has low self-esteem and finds school to be stressful and unrewarding is at greater risk. As a parent, you will need to be careful to watch for signs that your child may be in serious trouble, and ready to seek appropriate intervention when needed.

The Undiagnosed Teenager with Dyslexia

Often, very bright children are able to compensate for their dyslexia in the early school years, but cannot cope with the greater intellectual demands of secondary level schooling. Some common signs that your teenager may have dyslexia are:

- Your child must repeatedly read and reread material in order to understand it.
- Your child has extreme difficulty managing and keeping track of homework assignments and deadlines for his various classes.

- Your child repeatedly reports that he was unaware of assignments and deadlines because the teacher "never told" him what was required.
- Your child has unexpected difficulty with learning a foreign language.
- Your child struggles with higher math, such as algebra.
- There is a significant discrepancy between your child's school performance and scores on standardized tests, including College Board tests such as the PSAT.

If your child shows significant problems in any one of the above areas, it is a sign that he may have a previously undiagnosed learning disability. You should discuss these issues with him and also talk to parents of his classmates to find out whether their children are also having problems with the same subjects. Sometimes a problem with a math class or the first year of a foreign language can simply be the result of a poor teacher; poor grades in any subject can also occur with a teacher who is unusually strict in grading practices. If it is a "teacher" problem, usually other students and parents will have similar complaints. However, if the problems seem to be unusual or persistent, you should seek an evaluation for dyslexia or other learning barriers. The guidance counselor at school may be able to help arrange such testing, as well as to help plan your child's course schedule to better meet his needs.

Chapter 3

Getting a Diagnosis

Ten Things You Will Learn in This Chapter

- When you should seek help for your child.

- What kinds of professionals are qualified to diagnose dyslexia.

- Common tests used to diagnose dyslexia and what they mean.

- How a formal diagnosis might benefit your child.

- Some terms used to describe different types of dyslexia.

- Why some evaluators use different language to describe dyslexia.

- How to obtain evaluation for learning disabilities from your child's school.

- Why family members may resist testing.

- When a formal diagnosis may not be necessary.

- How dyslexia may manifest if your child is intellectually gifted.

Deciding to Seek Help

If you suspect that your child has dyslexia, you will probably want to seek testing and a diagnosis. The first step is to recognize that your child has a learning problem and that she will need extra help or intervention to overcome her difficulties. Coming to this point may be surprisingly difficult. Your child's own performance may be different from day to day, leading you to question whether there is any significant problem. Unfortunately, this inconsistency is part of the profile of dyslexia, as children with dyslexia are particularly susceptible to the effects of fatigue, stress, or frustration.

Fear of Labeling

Many parents are afraid that if their child is "labeled" with a learning disability, the label will do more harm than good. You may fear that your child will be placed in a special education classroom with children who have cognitive or emotional problems far worse than dyslexia, or that the diagnosis will prevent your child from having access to more challenging courses and enrichment opportunities. You may also be afraid that your child will be singled out and rejected by his peers. Your child may harbor similar fears. More than anything, she wants to be liked and accepted by her peers, and to be able to learn as quickly as they do and share in the same activities. Like you, she also fears being singled out or left behind.

Fortunately, many of these fears are unfounded. Public awareness has increased dramatically, and most people now understand that children with dyslexia are bright and capable. Teachers and school administrators will usually understand that your child may be struggling in one area but capable of doing advanced work in another. A diagnosis of dyslexia is often the first step toward structuring an educational program that will lead your child toward success. In fact, for a very bright child, testing of IQ and aptitude for dyslexia may also lead to qualification and placement in your school's program for gifted and talented youngsters. Once the learning disability is recognized, your child's innate strengths and potential might also become more apparent. In contrast, the failure to diagnose can leave your child struggling against an ever-increasing set of academic demands, with no real prospect of receiving help or understanding. Very few children can overcome dyslexia without specialized help and academic support.

Overcoming Resistance to Testing

You may find that when you discuss your child's problems with others, they may try to dissuade you from seeking a diagnosis. When you raise the issue with your child's teacher, she may try to reassure you that your child simply needs more time. She may seem to try to avoid any discussion of the subject, or actively discourage you from asking for testing, arguing that you do not want your child labeled with a disability.

You may also encounter surprising resistance from your family members. It is common for one parent to feel that the learning problems can be resolved with hard work and determination. Other family members may suggest that your child's problems stem from laziness, lack of motivation, or immaturity—and even try to blame your parenting style, arguing that your child simply needs more attention or discipline.

Again, you need to trust your instincts. Keep in mind that if you are mistaken in suspecting dyslexia, the best way to find out is through testing and diagnosis. Even if your child does not have dyslexia, an evaluation by a qualified professional may help you discover other issues that are at the root of your child's school problems.

When an Older Child Asks for Help

In some cases, your older child or teenager may be the one who asks for testing. Your child may find the academic demands in middle school and high school overwhelming, at least in some subject areas. He may have learned about dyslexia on his own, through Internet websites or by talking to other kids. In any case, he knows that he is struggling with material that seems easy for his peers. Your teenager may be afraid to bring up the subject of dyslexia at home. He may be embarrassed to let you know just how poorly he is doing at school, or he may be afraid that you will be angry or upset. It is important that you listen to your child and try to understand the reasons he feels he needs extra help. You might want to take a list of common dyslexia symptoms from this book or from a website, and ask your child to show you which problems on the list he feels apply to him. You may be surprised to learn that your child has been struggling for years, but has managed in the past to hide his problems through sheer determination and hard work. Your support and understanding is crucial;

for a child who has previously done well academically, an appropriate diagnosis can be the boost he needs to excel in high school and gain admittance into the college of his choice.

Is Diagnosis Always Necessary?

Some families are able to help their children without formal testing and diagnosis. Keep in mind that dyslexia is not a disease or mental defect, but a learning difference that usually requires that the child receive extra educational support. You don't need a prescription to enroll your child at a learning center or hire a tutor, and the same multisensory teaching methods that are best for children with dyslexia will also tend to help other children, as they are geared to reach multiple learning styles.

If you homeschool, or if your child is attending a school with a flexible and understanding staff, you may find that his needs can be well addressed without going through the process of a formal diagnosis of a learning disability. However, diagnostic testing will help you better understand your child and may guide you to make better choices. Ideally, testing should give you a map of your child's strong and weak points, and a set of recommendations as to how best to meet his educational needs.

DID YOU KNOW?

Research shows that approximately 15 percent of all school children have dyslexia. However, only 5 percent of school children are identified as having a learning disability. The other 10 percent are missed because teachers fail to recognize that they are struggling, or that their academic or behavior problems are connected to specific difficulties with learning.

A diagnosis of dyslexia or a related learning disability will also give you and your child important legal rights. If your child is in public school, the diagnosis will require the school authorities to work with you to design an Individualized Education Program (IEP) to meet your child's needs. You will be entitled to have a voice in the process and to attend regular meetings to discuss and monitor your child's progress and make modifications to the IEP as needed.

It's possible that a diagnosis could also prompt your child's school to offer him appropriate modifications and accommodations to enable him to experience success in school. For example, he might be allowed extra time on tests or be allowed to use a calculator. These modifications help level the playing field so your child is able to keep pace with his classmates.

How Dyslexia Is Diagnosed

There is no single test for dyslexia that all experts use, or any single agreed-upon standard for testing. There is not even a definition of dyslexia that is uniformly accepted. The symptoms and characteristics of dyslexia vary significantly from one individual to the next, and the range of difficulties can vary from being quite mild to extremely severe. Some experts define dyslexia broadly to include a range of common learning difficulties, whereas others use different names and categories to describe the various academic, social, and behavioral issues that may accompany dyslexia.

Dyslexia by Any Other Name

The process of diagnosis is complicated by the fact that experts in different fields often prefer using different names to describe the symptoms they see. For a specialist, the term "dyslexia" seems overbroad when more precise terminology can be used to describe individual symptoms. Some experts might divide dyslexia into various subtypes; others might elect to call it something else entirely, such as "Developmental Reading Disorder." The specific label attached to your child's learning problems may depend on who is doing the labeling; a medical doctor, for example, is likely to use different terminology than a learning specialist at your child's school. While this can seem terribly confusing, it is important to stay focused on what the evaluators tell you about your child's learning needs.

Who Can Diagnose Dyslexia?

Dyslexia is diagnosed by a specialist who is trained and qualified in the assessment of learning disabilities. This may include:

- Clinical or educational psychologists
- School psychologists
- Neuropsychologists
- Learning disabilities specialists

- Medical doctors with training and experience in the assessment of learning problems

Your child's evaluation might also include examination by other medical specialists. An audiologist might be involved in determining whether your child has problems with hearing or processing the sounds of language. A developmental optometrist might be needed to determine whether your child has vision difficulties that are contributing to his reading problems. Even if your child has 20/20 vision, reading might be hampered because of difficulties with near point vision, tracking, or eye teaming. A neurologist may be involved to test for problems that may stem from brain damage or problems with brain function beyond dyslexia. If your child has problems regulating his behavior or sustaining attention, a child psychologist or psychiatrist may be consulted to evaluate for Attention Deficit Disorder (ADD or ADHD) or other psychiatric and emotional problems.

The purpose of all this testing is not only to determine whether your child has dyslexia, but also to consider and rule out the possibility of other problems that may contribute to his learning difficulties. Your child may have a number of different issues, some of which may be easier to treat than others.

DOES THIS SOUND LIKE YOUR CHILD?

Your child's teacher may suggest that he be tested for ADHD because of classroom behavior problems. If your child is having problems with reading or writing, it is crucial that he also be tested for dyslexia and other learning disabilities. Medication commonly used for ADHD may seem to help your child pay attention in class, but it will not help him learn to read or resolve a learning disability.

Early Diagnosis and Screening

Because dyslexia is primarily diagnosed through tests measuring skills related to reading and reading readiness, it is not possible to reliably diagnose a child who is too young to start school. Many common symptoms of dyslexia, such as letter reversals in writing, are also part of normal childhood development. Children grow and learn at different rates. Even though most children can learn to read at age six, many are not ready to learn to read until age seven or eight. That is why reading instruction in schools generally continues through the primary grades, from kindergarten through grade three.

This does not mean that your child cannot be helped, however. There are many reasons why a young child may be struggling in school, but extra support and reading instruction will help all children who are falling behind. A young child can be screened for early signs of dyslexia, and you can plan age-appropriate early interventions if indicated. If you are concerned about early signs of dyslexia in your preschool-age child (age three to five), you can also provide extra support at home to help build reading readiness skills.

Measurements and Labels

There are several different tests that may be used to evaluate your child. They are not necessarily specific to dyslexia, but when combined they help provide a good picture of your child's development.

Wechsler Intelligence Scale

An evaluator will often start with an IQ test to determine your child's overall ability level. One of the most common tests used is the Wechsler Intelligence Scale for Children (WISC III or WISC IV). This test is favored because it breaks down scores into two scales, Verbal and Performance, which in turn each consist of various subtests. The Verbal Scale measures language expression, comprehension, listening, and the ability to apply these skills to solving problems. The Performance Scale assesses nonverbal problem solving, perceptual organization, speed, and visual-motor proficiency. It includes tasks like puzzles, picture analysis, imitating designs with blocks, and copying. This test is given orally, by an evaluator working individually with your child, so your child does not have to know how to read to score well on the test.

DID YOU KNOW?

You may be told that dyslexia is a medical term and that you will need a medical doctor to diagnose it. This is not true. Your child's pediatrician may be able to make recommendations and refer you to appropriate specialists, but she will not be able to make a determination as to whether or not your child has dyslexia.

By looking at the scores on various subtests, the evaluator will see a pattern of strengths and weaknesses. This sort of testing is extremely valuable for all children and can be used to indicate a wide variety of learning disabilities. Dyslexia is indicated as a possible diagnosis if the subtests show that a child has particular weaknesses in areas normally associated with dyslexia—such as with verbal fluency, short-term auditory memory (digit span), or speed of processing information.

WISC testing will also provide a "full-scale" IQ—the number that results from combining the results of the Verbal and Performance scales. This is useful in evaluating overall cognitive ability and making recommendations for education and therapy. However, caution should be used in interpreting these results as a measure of your child's intellectual capacity. A very bright child may have a lower-than-expected IQ result due to poor performance on some of the subtests. If a child with a WISC IQ score in the average range scores particularly high on some of the subtests, further testing with other IQ tests is needed to assess for possible giftedness. Your child's emotional state and attitude toward testing could also result in poor performance on this test.

Achievement Tests
Your child will also be given achievement tests to measure reading performance. The specific tests will

vary depending on the preferences of the evaluator and the age of your child. Younger children will be given tests that measure prereading and early reading skills, such as simple word recognition tests. Older children may be given tests that measure sentence reading, oral fluency, and reading comprehension.

These tests are not the same as the standardized tests that are used in schools to assess classroom performance. Group standardized tests are not valid for measuring individual ability levels, because they are designed for purposes of comparing the overall achievement of large groups of children. Although your child's scores on standardized tests may be a relevant piece of information to include in an evaluation, these tests are not a reliable way to diagnose learning disabilities.

Specialized Tests for Dyslexia

There are also some specialized tests geared to measuring problems commonly associated with dyslexia. For example, a child's ability to parse out the sounds of language can be measured with tests of phonemic awareness. Your child may be asked to read a set of "nonwords"—that is, invented words with no real meaning such as SLIMP or HIFE. He may also be asked to say whether certain words rhyme, or to break apart words by their sounds, such as to say the word "bent" without the "n" sound. There are also tests given that assess word retrieval skills and auditory and verbal processing speed, such as tests of Rapid Automatic Naming, which require the child to quickly read aloud the names of letters or numbers presented on a chart or graph. Short-term memory, or digit span, might also be tested. These tests ask children to remember and repeat a short sequence of letters or numbers, or to identify a sequence of letters, numbers, or pictures after briefly viewing a picture or card with the same sequence.

Types of Dyslexia

When there is a diagnosis of dyslexia, it is often classified into one of several subtypes. These subtypes are basically labels for the pattern of symptoms that emerged through testing, and the labels are in part dependent on the evaluator's choice of tests to administer. Some of the common subtypes are:

- **Dysphonetic dyslexia** (also called dysphonesia; phonological dyslexia; or auditory dyslexia): This form is characterized by difficulties with word attack skills, including phonetic segmentation and blending. It can be identified by poor nonword reading skills; i.e., inability to decipher invented words with no real meaning used to test phonetic skills.

- **Dyseidetic dyslexia** (also called dyseidesia, surface dyslexia, or visual dyslexia): This is the term used when testing shows your child has a good ability to sound out words, but reading is labored. Children with this type have difficulty learning to recognize whole words visually, and have problems deciphering words that do not follow regular phonetic rules. Spelling is highly phonetic, for example writing "skul" for "school."

- **Naming-speed deficits** (also called semantic dyslexia, dysnomia, or anomia): This subtype of dyslexia is diagnosed primarily from poor performance on tests of rapid automatic naming. Children with naming speed deficits have difficulty with word retrieval. They may hesitate in speech, or frequently substitute a mistaken word for what they mean, such as saying "tornado" when they mean "volcano." They may also frequently use generic words (i.e., "thing," or "place") instead of specific nouns; or they may resort to descriptive phrases. (i.e., "the eating thing" rather than "spoon").

- **Double-deficit:** Double-deficit dyslexia is a label attached to children who have both the phonological and the naming-speed subtypes. These children are thought to have a particularly severe and persistent form of dyslexia.

Many children have symptoms that overlap more than one of the various subtypes, and are not able to be easily categorized. Research suggests that approximately 60 percent of children with dyslexia have the dysphonetic form, while about 10 percent have the dyseidetic form.

Requesting an Evaluation from Your Child's School

In the United States, the federal Individuals with Disabilities in Education Act (IDEA) requires that public schools provide testing, without charge to the parents, whenever there is reason to suspect a learning disability. Even if your child is in private school, you are entitled to these services from the public school district. In many cases the evaluation will be initiated at the request of a teacher or a school administrator familiar with your child. However, if you suspect that your child has dyslexia, you can request testing directly. Be sure to put your request in writing and send it to the school principal.

Beginning the Process

You should not limit your request to a test for dyslexia, as the law requires that your child be assessed "in all areas related to the suspected disability" and it is possible that some of your child's problems may stem from another related condition. Rather, your letter should briefly state the reasons you suspect a learning disability, and then request full evaluation of your child. The letter should also say that you consent to evaluation under the terms of the Individuals with Disabilities Act. Be sure the letter is dated and is signed by you, and keep a copy for your records.

DID YOU KNOW?

You may be told that your child is too young to be tested for dyslexia, or that there is no test for dyslexia that can be given. If your child is old enough to attend school, this is not true. Even though a firm diagnosis may not be possible, federal law requires that the school evaluate your child for learning disabilities, and specifically includes "dyslexia" among the types of learning disabilities covered.

The federal law requires the school to complete an evaluation of your child within sixty days after you make the request, unless your state has set a different time frame through its own laws.

If the evaluation shows that your child has dyslexia or a related disability, the law requires that the school provide whatever special education services are needed because of the learning disability. You are legally entitled to inspect and review all educational records that the school relies on in making its determination, so you will be able to see the specific results of whatever diagnostic testing is completed by the school.

Requesting   an   Independent   Educational Evaluation

If you are not satisfied with the results of the school's evaluation, you may request an Independent Educational Evaluation (IEE) by a qualified evaluator of your choosing. The school must provide you with information about where the independent educational evaluation may be obtained. The IEE will be done at public expense, unless the school initiates a proceeding before an impartial hearing officer to oppose the second evaluation.

DID YOU KNOW?

If you are confused about procedures, you can get assistance from your state's Parent Training and

Information (PTI) center. Every state has at least one PTI; these are agencies funded by the U.S. Department of Education to provide training and information to parents of children with disabilities.

The school may ask you the reasons that you object to the initial determination; however, you are not required by law to give an explanation. Of course, like the initial request, you should make any request for an IEE in writing and keep copies of all correspondence.

Keep in mind that the goal of the evaluation under IDEA is to determine whether your child has a learning disability that requires special education services. You should not make the mistake of seeking further evaluation simply because you do not like the label or terminology used in your child's evaluation, as it is very common for evaluators to use words other than "dyslexia" to describe the same problem.

Overlapping and Related Conditions

The results of testing may indicate that your child has a learning disability other than dyslexia. In some cases, the learning disability may be the same thing as dyslexia. For example, the evaluation may conclude that your child has a "Developmental Reading Disorder" or "Phonological Processing Disorder." These phrases are merely different ways of describing dyslexia or a subtype. It is also very common for children with dyslexia to be diagnosed as having Attention Deficit Disorder, Central Auditory Processing Disorder (APD or CAPD), or a visual processing issue. These are different from dyslexia, but there is substantial overlap in symptoms. That is, in many cases diagnosis of these conditions will be made based on the same symptoms that support a diagnosis of dyslexia.

For example, dyslexia is primarily a problem with processing of language, and reading problems are often accompanied by problems with using and understanding language. It is possible for a child to have an auditory processing disorder without dyslexia, but when a child has both the auditory processing issues and difficulty with reading, they probably are simply different manifestations of the same underlying language processing problem. The real issue is that the child needs help with understanding the sounds of language.

Similarly, Attention Deficit Disorder is generally characterized by high distractibility, difficulty staying "on task," and a variety of related behavioral problems. A child who cannot read and is feeling confused or frustrated in the classroom is likely to manifest the same sort of symptoms.

A BETTER PARENTING PRACTICE

Find out exactly what symptoms support each diagnosis, and think about what you have observed in your child. If the diagnosis does not make sense to you, it may be mistaken. Focus on what sort of help your child actually needs, not on the label that is given to his symptoms.

However, it is also possible that a child will have additional symptoms or problems that will support a dual diagnosis. For example, difficulty with reading will not cause a child to be hyperactive, but many children with dyslexia also have the hyperactive form of ADHD. Solving one problem will not help unless the other is also addressed.

Dyslexia and the Gifted Child

As a result of testing, you may be surprised to learn that your child is intellectually gifted. It is very common for the difficulties associated with dyslexia to mask your child's true potential. Your child may have a brilliant mind, but his difficulties with verbal and written language have prevented him from expressing his thoughts in a way that others could understand. The combination of intellectual giftedness with learning disabilities is actually quite common. Gifted children have learning disabilities at least as often as other children. Research has shown that children who are highly or profoundly gifted often have predominantly visual-spatial or right-brained learning styles; this puts them at particularly high risk for dyslexia.

On the other hand, your child's strong intellectual abilities may also make it difficult to get a firm diagnosis of dyslexia. Test results may show that your child has some, but not all, of the common symptoms of dyslexia; or your child simply might not score badly enough on any of the tests to support a diagnosis. A close look at scores on various sub-tests may reveal signs of specific learning barriers that are holding your child back.

Chapter 4

Getting Help at School

Ten Things You Will Learn in This Chapter

- What help the school may offer before your child is diagnosed with dyslexia.

- How Response to Intervention (RTI) may be used to identify children with learning disabilities.

- What happens at an IEP meeting.

- Some elements of a good IEP plan.

- How to prepare for your child's IEP meeting

- How the standard of a "Free and Appropriate Education" may limit options available to your child.

- What services are typically offered to children after qualifying for special education services.

- Why a placement in special education may not serve your child's needs.

- Some common classroom modifications that may help your child.

- How technology can be used to allow your child to keep up in a regular classroom.

When Your Child First Falls Behind

Even without a formal diagnosis of dyslexia, your child might be offered special services or tutoring at his school to help him catch up with early reading skills during the primary grades. Early intervention programs are a way to reach many children who are lagging behind their peers in the hope that prompt, short-term intervention will be effective to allow the child to perform well in a regular classroom.

Reading Recovery

Reading Recovery is a short-term program of one-on-one tutoring for struggling first graders, geared to rapidly bringing students up to grade level. The program is well-established and has been used in the United States since 1984. It is aimed at the lowest-achieving students, who each receive a half-hour daily lesson for twelve to twenty weeks with a specially trained teacher. Lessons include reading familiar stories, working with letters or words using magnetic letters, writing a story, and reading a new book. The lessons focus on phonics as well as problem-solving strategies and reading comprehension, and are individualized for each child, building on strengths and responding to the child's growing abilities. As soon as the student is able to read independently at a level equivalent to average students in his class, he is removed from the program and another student takes his place.

However, Reading Recovery is not designed to address specific learning disabilities such as dyslexia, and it should not be used as a substitute for special education services. If your child does not progress with this program, services will typically be withdrawn at the end of twenty weeks. At that point, the process should begin to qualify your child for more specialized services.

Response to Intervention

Response to Intervention (RTI) is a new approach designed to help identify students at risk for learning disabilities and work with all students to promote educational success. This approach may be used by a school as part of their process for identifying and evaluating your child under the provisions of the 2004 amendments to the Individuals with Disabilities Education Act (IDEA). However, there is no formal definition of the RTI process and each school may implement it differently.

In general, RTI begins with generalized screening of all students to identify the lowest-performing students. Students who show signs of learning difficulties receive a series of increasingly intensive interventions, moving from special tutoring and small group instruction to more targeted, individualized interventions as needed. The intervention process includes systematic monitoring of each student's progress. If your child is assigned to RTI and does not show improvement, or a "response," she might then be qualified for special education services under IDEA.

A BETTER PARENTING PRACTICE

A survey shows that 44 percent of parents waited a year or more after noticing their child was struggling at school before seeking help. You do not need a

formal diagnosis of a learning disability in order to
start trying to find help for your child. If your child
is doing poorly or seems frustrated with school,
he should have reading support or intervention as
soon as possible.

The benefit of RTI is that it enables schools to begin
delivering services to students without requiring formal
evaluation and diagnosis of learning disabilities. The
law allows the evidence gained from tracking the student through the program to be used to establish the
existence of a learning disability. This can avoid delays
that parents typically encounter when requesting formal evaluation.

However, use of RTI can also delay full evaluation,
and it would not provide the comprehensive information
about your child's learning needs that might be gained
with formalized testing. Also, RTI does not afford the
specific legal protections and benefits that your child
would get with an IEP. If you believe that RTI is not
appropriate for your child, you should request formal
evaluation under IDEA. Legally, the school cannot use
the RTI process as an excuse to deny or delay a formal
evaluation for special education.

The Individualized Education Program (IEP)

Under IDEA, your child will qualify for special education services if she is determined to have dyslexia
or another of thirteen listed disabilities, and if by
reason of that disability she needs special education
services in order to make progress in school and to

benefit from the general education program. Planning will begin with an Individualized Education Program (IEP) meeting, which must take place within thirty days of the determination of eligibility for services.

An IEP has two purposes. First, it sets reasonable learning goals for your child. Then, it outlines the services that the school district will provide and specifies where they will take place.

The IEP Meeting

As a parent, you are entitled to have input into the IEP decision-making process. The school must take steps to ensure that one or both parents are present at each IEP meeting and are given the opportunity to participate. This includes notifying you of the meeting early enough to enable you to attend, scheduling the meeting at a mutually agreed-upon time and place, and providing you with all the necessary information regarding the meeting and your rights as parents. Your child may also attend the meeting if you wish.

A BETTER PARENTING PRACTICE

You can improve the quality and effectiveness of your child's IEP meetings by bringing a buddy. Bring your spouse or a close family member if you can. Consider pairing up with another parent of a special needs child—offer to attend her IEP meetings if she will attend yours. Don't forget your child—as he grows older, he can learn useful self-advocacy skills by being an active participant in the IEP process.

Your child's IEP will be determined by a team that includes the following:

- The parents
- At least one of your child's regular classroom teachers;
- At least one special education teacher
- A representative of the school district who is qualified to provide or supervise special education services, knows the general education curriculum, and knows about the availability of school district resources
- A person who is qualified to interpret the instructional implications of evaluation results, such as a school psychologist
- Any individuals who have knowledge or special expertise regarding the student, including an advocate or private tutor, who may be invited to attend by either the school or the parent
- When appropriate, the student

Contents of IEP

The IEP should begin with a specific statement of your child's present levels of educational performance, and explain how your child's learning disability affects his involvement and progress in the general curriculum.

The IEP should then specify a set of objectively measurable annual goals, including benchmarks and short-term objectives. These goals should be directly related to the learning disability that qualifies your child for services.

IEP goals should be specific and directly related to your child's learning needs and achievement levels. For example, "Robert will increase oral reading skills to fifth-grade level as measured by the Gray Oral Reading Test" is measurable and specific; "Robert will work to improve reading fluency" is not. Make sure that goals are both reasonable in light of your child's present level of functioning and his expected grade level.

The IEP must also specify how your child's progress toward the annual goals will be measured, and regularly reported to you. You are entitled to regular progress reports at least as often as school report cards are issued.

Finally, the IEP must specify the services and modifications that will be provided to address each of your child's needs. The actual availability of services has no bearing on the IEP. That is, if a service is needed it must be written on the IEP; if the school district cannot directly provide the service, it must arrange for and fund the service to be provided by another agency.

Preparing for the Meeting

In order to advocate effectively for your child, you should plan and prepare in advance for the IEP meeting. If you are not ready, you are likely to find the process intimidating—you may arrive to find yourself confronting a roomful of teachers and school administrators, and find it difficult to express yourself or hold your ground.

Start by talking to your child. Ask her what is going well in school and what she would like to do better. Explain the purpose of the meeting, and ask your child whether she would like to attend.

Write a short description of your child, including a list of his strengths and weaknesses.

Include such items as hobbies, behavior at home, and relationship with family and friends. Focusing on your child's strengths, interests, and preferences will help develop an IEP that best meets his needs. Write out a list of your specific concerns and questions, and list your own recommendations or ideas for how to best meet your child's needs.

Write down some goals you would like to see your child achieve in the coming year.

Be sure that you know your options. Gather information about various programs offered within your school district, as well as any privately provided programs that may be appropriate for your child. Talk with your child's teacher, the district special education administrator, and other parents. Visit your child's classroom so that you can observe his present learning environment. If possible, visit potential programs that might be indicated for your child before the IEP meeting.

A BETTER PARENTING PRACTICE

The IEP meeting is a time to use teamwork to help your child, and create goals for the future—not to revisit or argue over past mistakes. At the meeting, show a positive outlook. Start by talking about some areas you know everyone will agree with; find common ground. Avoid speaking in absolutes, such as "always" or "never." Focus on your concerns about your child and specific needs, and use questions ("What if we tried . . . .?") to elicit suggestions from other IEP team members, rather than a declarative statement of a firm position.

Use this information to develop your ideal IEP to present at the meeting. Gather all available information that supports your position and your child's ideal IEP. This can include new information, such as an evaluation by someone outside the school district or a statement from your child's pediatrician.

Ask for a written list of the people the school plans to have at your child's IEP meeting. Let your school contact person know if you plan to bring others to the meeting as well. Try to find out in advance what school staff members are likely to recommend at the meeting. It is especially important for you to know what to expect from your child's teacher, as her opinions and suggestions will usually be given great deference. If possible, meet with the teacher in advance to go over your mutual concerns—things will go better if you and the teacher present a united front.

Invite appropriate people who can support your position to speak at the IEP meeting. This can be an experienced advocate, or a professional who has worked with your child, or someone who provides services that you would like your child to receive. If a key person cannot intend, have her prepare a written statement for you to read at the meeting. It is also a good idea to bring a support person, such as a friend or another parent, who can assist you by taking notes and helping you stay focused at the meeting.

DID YOU KNOW?

If you are unable to personally attend the meeting at your child's school, you can ask for an alternative to a face-to-face meeting, such as through telephone conference calls or video conferences.

Organize your materials in advance, and make photocopies of any important documents or exhibits (such as samples of your child's school work) that you are bringing, so that you can distribute these to the other people at the meeting. You may want to assemble a portfolio of your child's work, and keep a binder with all school documents, reports and information related to the IEP process. These can be updated from year to year.

FAPE—Free and Appropriate Education

As a parent, you naturally want what is best for your child. You want your child to receive the best education possible and to maximize his learning potential. You may have a specific program or therapy in mind that you think your child needs. However, the law does not require that school administrators provide the best possible interventions for your child; rather, the school is only required to provide a "free and appropriate education"—commonly designated as FAPE.

FAPE means that the school is required to provide individualized instruction with sufficient support services to enable your child to benefit educationally from the instruction. In other words, the school must provide the minimal level of support that is adequate to allow your child to learn. The Supreme Court has held that this standard is met with services that are reasonably calculated to enable the child to achieve passing marks and advance from grade to grade.

Many children with dyslexia are extremely bright, and often their pattern of weaknesses and strengths leaves them highly functional in many areas, even though they struggle in others. For example, your child may read very slowly, but with excellent comprehension, and she may have a strong ability to retain information learned from oral instruction and class demonstrations. Through hard work and determination, your child may be able to keep up in class and generally earn Bs and Cs in class work. With such a child, you may find it difficult to qualify for school services, even with a diagnosis of dyslexia—the school may take the position that the dyslexia is mild and does not affect her ability to learn.

Even if your child does qualify, you may find that the services offered are not adequate. Through formal testing or your own observations, you may realize that your child is intellectually gifted and capable of learning at an accelerated pace, if only the reading barrier were addressed. You will want to find a corrective approach to dyslexia—one that is geared to eliminating barriers and employs a fast-paced instructional methodology— but the school will see its obligation to be far more limited in scope. In fact, if your child does receive special education services, you may find that as soon as he progresses to what you consider to be a level of minimal proficiency, the services are withdrawn.

You can't change the law, but understanding the concept of FAPE will help you know how to frame your arguments when dealing with school authorities. Use language like "appropriate" and "adequate" when asking for services, and highlight your child's weakest skill areas. For example, if your child is earning Bs in the regular fourth-grade classroom, but standardized tests show that he is reading on a first-grade level, work toward an IEP that will specify efforts to be taken to help him learn to read at grade level. Do not let your child's strong compensation skills overshadow his need for specific remediation in areas of weakness.

Typical Special Education Services

Usually, a child with dyslexia will have an IEP that will provide that she will spend most of her day in the regular classroom, but also spend part of her day in a resource room with a special education teacher. Resource rooms provide support for children for a small portion of the school day. Class size is typically limited to eight to fourteen students, allowing individualized attention and small group instruction. The resource room typically serves the needs of children with a variety of learning difficulties. Your child may also spend a specified amount of time each week working with a speech and language therapist or an occupational therapist.

DID YOU KNOW?

Research shows that children placed in special education often fare worse over time than their counterparts in regular classrooms, frequently showing an overall deterioration in reading skills rather than an improvement. This may stem from practices that deprive children of exposure to grade-level language arts instruction while they are receiving remedial reading instruction.

If warranted, the IEP may specify that your child be placed in a special education classroom for all of her studies. IDEA requires that services be given in the "least restrictive environment," meaning that your child should not be removed from the regular classroom for more time than absolutely necessary to provide supportive educational services. Full-time placement in a special education class is rarely a good choice for children with dyslexia, as it often segregates them to learn with children with much more severe intellectual and emotional problems. If such a placement is being considered for your child, be sure to visit the special education classroom; some schools do have skilled and innovative teachers who are able to bring out the best in their students. While you should be wary of a full-time special education placement, keep an open mind until you have met the teacher and have seen for yourself what type of students will be in the classroom with your child.

ADA and 504 Accommodations

In addition to the provisions of IDEA discussed before, your child may also be entitled to accommodations or classroom modifications under the Americans with Disabilities Act of 1990 (ADA) or Section 504 of the Rehabilitation Act of 1973. These laws protect your child from discrimination on the basis of her learning disability. This may be a good alternative if your child has been diagnosed with dyslexia, but has difficulty qualifying for services because she is not "behind enough" and does not seem to need tutoring or special education in order to keep up in class. Even if your child does qualify for services, you might also prefer the ADA/504 protections if you do not agree with the educational plan and goals specified by the IEP, but still want to obtain modifications for your child.

DID YOU KNOW?

Some common 504 accommodations are extended time on tests or assignments, peer assistance with note-taking, extra set of textbooks for home use, computer-aided instruction, enlarged print, rearranging class schedules, preferred seating assignments, oral testing, or use of tape recorder in lieu of taking notes.

The difference between protections under ADA/504 and IDEA is that your child does not have to demonstrate a need for special education services in order to receive ADA/504 accommodations. On the other hand, with ADA/504, he will not have an IEP or be given specialized tutoring or educational services. What your child can get via the anti-discrimination laws is the right to use assistive devices, such as a calculator or keyboard, or modifications such as extended time on exams or an exam reader. Of course, you need to be able to show that your child needs these services to overcome his specific disability-related limitations; however, usually the diagnosis of dyslexia will suffice.

Although your child is legally entitled to "reasonable" accommodations, the law does not specify what is reasonable. This is something that may be determined by the school in accordance with its practices in similar cases, or it may be developed over time through trial and error.

Suggested Classroom Modifications

Modifications should be tailored to your child's specific needs, and they may vary in different settings or with different classes. For example, if your child has auditory discrimination problems, she may need to be seated closer to the front of the room in a class with a soft-spoken teacher, but may have no problems in another class where the teacher has a louder and more commanding demeanor. A child who has difficulty writing may need extra time to complete written essays or exams, but have no difficulty with worksheets or multiple-choice exams that merely require checking or circling the correct answer.

Some common accommodations are:

- **Extra time.** Your child might need extended time on just about anything: on written homework, on oral tasks requiring a rapid response, or simply moving from one task to another in class.
- **Alternative assignments.** Your child might need to substitute all or part of an assignment with an alternative project or task; for example, a science project could be modified to allow your child to build a model in lieu of writing a paper.
- **Assistive technology.** Your child may do better on written assignments if she is allowed to use a laptop computer or keyboard to type them, rather than turn in handwritten work. In addition to utilities such as a spell checker that are standard on most computers, your child may benefit from more sophisticated software, like predictive-text programs, text-to-speech utilities, dictation software; or handheld devices like an electronic spelling dictionary or calculator.
- **E-books, recorded books, and multimedia.** Your child may do better if some or all of his assignments can be accessed through audio or visual formats. In some cases, equivalent information in textbooks may also be available in video or computer CD-ROM format.

- **Changes to classroom seating arrangement**.
  Your child may do better if seated closer to
  the teacher, or in an area that is shielded from
  distractions.
- **Modifications to curriculum.** Your child may
  need modifications to expected curriculum, such
  as a shorter spelling list or a spelling list made up
  of easier words.

Keep in mind that the ultimate goal is to maximize
your child's ability to learn by eliminating learning barriers, and making sure that assignments are within his
capacity to complete and to master. You do not want to
make things too easy for your child, but your child will
be discouraged and soon give up if every assignment
ends in frustration and failure.

Audio Books and Visual Aids
Your child may also be able to keep up with assigned
reading and improve his own fluency and comprehension skills by listening to books on tape or CD, or reading e-books along with a text-to-speech device. A wide
variety of literature is available in audio format; your
child can improve fluency and reading speed by reading
the text while simultaneously listening to audio, or he
can keep up with grade-level reading that is beyond his
own reading capacity by relying on listening alone. For
books that are not available commercially in an audio
format, including assigned textbooks, your child may
qualify for services from Recording for the Blind &

Dyslexic. This requires a small membership fee and use of a specialized listening device.

DID YOU KNOW?

Recording for the Blind & Dyslexic (RFB&D) was established in 1948 to provide recorded textbooks to veterans blinded in World War II. Today, RFB&D has a catalog of more than 500,000 titles. More than 70 percent of its members have been identified as having a learning disability.

Your child may also find it helpful to use videos or DVDs to supplement classroom reading; for instance, watching movie versions of novels and plays that are assigned reading. Educational videos or CDs with multimedia content may also supplement the content of textbooks on any number of subjects; your highly visual child is likely to learn, retain, and understand far more from watching a documentary about the Civil War than reading a chapter in his history book. Keep in mind that if your child does not read comfortably at grade level, audiovisual media is his primary means to accessing more advanced topics and subject matter. Your child is a capable learner; while reading remediation is important, his reading difficulties should not prevent him from studying and learning advanced materials when he can get information from alternative sources.

Chapter 5

Reading Programs for Dyslexia

Ten Things You Will Learn in This Chapter

- What kind of tutoring services may help your child.
- The characteristics of Orton-Gillingham tutoring.
- What to look for in a tutor for your child.
- What you can expect from phonemic awareness training.
- Expected results with phonics-based tutoring.
- What strategies are best for developing reading fluency.
- About new research that supports methods that connect meaning, appearance, and sounds of words.
- Some common reading programs used by many schools.
- How mental imagery can enhance reading comprehension.
- An explanation of the Lindamood-Bell programs for dyslexia.

When Your Child Needs Extra Support

Although dyslexia affects your child in many ways, you are likely to find that learning to read is the primary and most significant barrier. There is a confusing array of options and programs that may be recommended for your child. Many schools have now adopted excellent text series that provide a strong emphasis on phonics instruction for general use with all children in the classroom. However, although these reading programs may provide a good foundation, children with dyslexia usually need more specialized intervention. You may find that your child's school offers a specialized curriculum targeted toward struggling readers, and if you are fortunate your child will do well with school services. However, if your child continues to struggle, you will want to learn more about the programs offered by the school or seek help outside of school on your own.

You may consider enrolling your child in an after-school tutoring center such as Sylvan Learning Centers, Kumon, or Score! Educational Centers. This might be a good interim approach if your child is having difficulty at school but not faring badly enough to qualify for extra services, or if you are uncertain as to what sort of program is most appropriate for your child. Such programs are readily available and will provide tutoring directly targeted to your child's area of academic difficulty, usually within a small group setting. These centers may also provide good supplemental support in addition to other therapy or teaching that your child may be receiving, or help your child catch up after he has achieved minimal proficiency with a more specialized program. However, these centers are not geared to children with learning disabilities, and the tutors they employ do not have specific training in how to reach children with dyslexia. If your child is not happy in such a program or does not seem to be making progress, it is a good sign that more specialized intervention is needed.

Specialized Programs to Develop Phonemic Awareness
In order to decode text, a beginning reader must be able to correctly identify the sounds that make up words. A phoneme is the smallest unit of sound which can differentiate word meaning in a given language. There are forty-four phonemes in the English language, represented by the twenty-six letters of our alphabet. Phonemic awareness is the ability to recognize and isolate the individual phonemes in a word. For example, the word *sent* has four phonemes—the sounds represented by each of its letters. An individual with good phonemic awareness is able to differentiate among and manipulate the four sounds. Phonemes are not the same as letters: the word *toad* has only three phonemes, though it has four letters; the "oa" is a digraph that represents a single sound, the long vowel.

Phonemic Awareness and Dyslexia
Most children with dyslexia will score poorly on tests designed to measure phonemic awareness, and they will have corresponding difficulty using phonetic strategies to decode words. Children do not develop phonemic awareness naturally, as it is not inherent in the process

of listening to sounds of words. It is not necessary to break up words into separate sounds to hear or to speak them; to the ear, a single-syllable word seems like one continuous bundle of sound. Children gain phonemic awareness through exposure to print and the concept that letters represent sounds. Phonemic awareness is a learned skill; as children start to learn to read, their early attempts at decoding reinforces their rudimentary skills.

However, children with reading delays are not able to bolster their phonetic understanding through reading experience, and they will tend to fall farther behind their peers as time goes on. For this reason, programs to help children with reading difficulties often include specific training in phonemic awareness. These programs may be helpful to very young readers to help them with beginning reading skills, and many researchers hope that intensive training in phonemic awareness will help children overcome dyslexia.

A BETTER PARENTING PRACTICE

You can help your young child develop phonemic awareness skills at home by drawing his attention to letters and their sounds, and playing games involving manipulation of sounds, such as pig Latin, and teaching rhyming games and songs, such as the "Name Game."

However, such training should begin early. The National Reading Panel reported in 2000 that phonemic awareness training was more effective for children in preschool and kindergarten than for children above first grade level. Studies also showed mixed results for children with reading disabilities like dyslexia, perhaps because the inherent differences in their developing brains make it more difficult for them to learn these skills.

Fast ForWord Language

One therapy geared to developing phonemic awareness skills is *Fast ForWord Language*, a product of the Scientific Learning Corporation. This program uses special computer software which stretches out the sounds of language and provides children with listening practice in order to build phonological understanding and awareness. Your child plays a series of computer games, and as her ability to distinguish sounds improves, the software gradually increases difficulty and rate of speech, until your child either reaches a plateau in development or attains the highest level of mastery built into the software program.

DID YOU KNOW?

An alternative approach to building listening skills is *Earobics*, which also uses a computer game format. This software is available for home use and does not require special training to use. This program will also provide your child with extra practice learning to distinguish language sounds and relate them to letters and words.

The *Fast ForWord* program is very intense; students work with the computer for 100 minutes a day, five days a week, for four to eight weeks under the guidance of a trained clinician. Research shows that the program produces significant gains in phonemic awareness among children with weak skills at the outset of training, but results are mixed as to how well these gains transfer to other reading skills, such as word recognition, or whether children do better with this approach over time than with more conventional teaching methods. Because the program does not include direct reading instruction, it must be followed up with other teaching.

Building Decoding Skills with Phonics-Based Tutoring

Most primary-level reading programs for dyslexia are based on teaching phonics more intensively and thoroughly than is done in the regular classroom. Some of these programs teach phonics in isolation, and some focus on teaching phonetic elements in conjunction with other strategies to help with word recognition, spelling, fluency, and comprehension. Any phonics-based program will provide your child with some guidance as to understanding the sounds of language, the correspondence between letters and sounds, and segmenting (breaking apart) and blending (putting together) individual sounds to make words. However, the particular approach to teaching may vary, especially as to the sequence and pace of instruction.

Orton-Gillingham Approach

A widely recommended method for individual-ized tutoring of students with dyslexia is the Orton-Gillingham (O-G) approach. This is not a single pro-gram, but a model for teaching developed by dyslexia researcher Samuel T. Orton and psychologist Anna Gill-ingham in the 1930s. Dr. Orton saw dyslexia as being rooted in the tendency to reverse or transpose letters and coined the term "strephosymbolia" (twisted sym-bols) to describe the condition. He advocated including tracing and writing practice along with teaching of let-ters and sounds, so that the child's memory of the phys-ical movements associated with forming letters would eliminate confusion about the shape and appearance of the letters. Dr. Gillingham added to Dr. Orton's "multi-sensory" approach by creating a system for teaching the entire structure of written English by teaching letters and letter groups (called "phonograms") and their cor-responding sounds.

Characteristics of Orton-Gillingham

With the O-G approach, the teacher begins by presenting the most common consonants and vowels, one or two at a time. Each letter is taught using mul-tisensory methods, so that the child links how the let-ter looks with how it sounds and how it feels to form the letter. Some tutors have the child trace the letter in sand, write it in the air using large motions, or run their finger over fine sandpaper or textured carpet. After a child learns individual letters, the teacher moves on to consonant blends and letter combinations. Advanced students will study the rules of English language, syllable patterns, and how to use roots, prefixes, and suffixes to study words.

There are dozens of different reading methods that incorporate the basic principles of the O-G approach. Each method has differences in specific technique and manner of presentation, but all are characterized by the following elements:

- **Multisensory teaching:** Instruction involves interaction between what the student is seeing, hearing, and feeling in forming speech and writing. Language elements are reinforced by having the student listen, speak, read, and write.
- **Phonics-based:** Instruction focuses on teaching individual sounds of letters or letter combinations, rather than teaching whole words or word families.
- **Sequential:** Concepts are taught in a specifically designed order, beginning with the easiest and most basic, and moving on to more difficult material.
- **Structured, systematic, and cumulative:** Lessons are organized with specific patterns and activities, following a familiar routine. Each new lesson includes review of previously learned material, and concepts are reinforced through practice or repetition.

Finding a Qualified Orton-Gillingham Tutor

Many teachers and tutors have training in O-G methods and can provide help to your child. Your child's school may provide tutoring without charge, or you may choose to hire a private tutor. You should ask your tutor whether she has specific certifications, the name of the program or organization where she received her training, and the number of hours of training she has had. There are no "official" standards for teacher training in O-G methods, but there are several reputable organizations such as the nonprofit Academy of Orton-Gillingham Practitioners and Educators that provide professional training. The qualifications of your child's tutor may range from merely having watched a training video for a few hours, to having completed a short course of one or two days, to several hundred hours of course work and practice.

O-G tutoring is also available free of charge in many states through 32nd Degree Masonic Learning Centers, a charity of the Scottish Rite Masons; these centers have now provided services to more than 5,000 school children.

Effectiveness of O-G Teaching

Because O-G is so well-established, many educators assume that has been proven over time to be effective for dyslexia. However, most support is anecdotal—despite widespread use of such methods for almost seventy years, the Florida Center for Reading Research reported in 2006 that it was unable to find any formal empirical studies of the O-G approach. The Masonic Learning Centers tracked more than 213 students over two years and reported that the children improved significantly with their ability to decode nonsense words (a good test of phonetic knowledge) and with reading comprehension, but showed only minimal progress and remained below-average on tests of their ability to recognize real words in print.

The O-G emphasis on phonetic decoding is geared to beginning level readers. Because most children with dyslexia have difficulty with sequencing and with processing the sounds of language, an O-G teacher is working to build your child's skills in his weakest areas. Even with multisensory teaching, a good deal of drill, repetition, and practice is needed to cement the knowledge. It is reasonable for you to expect to see steady progress with your young child, but unlikely that he will progress by leaps and bounds. Although reports of progress rates are extremely variable, it is reasonable to expect about eighteen months of growth in reading ability for every twelve months of instruction, and to expect tutoring to continue for two to three years.

A BETTER PARENTING PRACTICE

Tutoring can be hard work for your child, but with a good teacher it can also be fun. Your child will do best with reading instruction that builds both skill and the desire to read increasingly complex materials. Look for a teacher who provides encouragement and finds ways to create successful reading experiences for your child.

Keep in mind that no one approach can meet every child's needs. Because O-G is so well-established, parents are sometimes discouraged from seeking other help if their child does not seem to benefit from the lessons, on the rationale that O-G is the "best" method. It is important to support your child's teacher and her efforts to help your child. However, if your child is frustrated or seems to be making little or no progress after several months of tutoring, it may be best to look for a different teacher or approach.

Phono-Graphix—An Alternative Phonics-Based Strategy

Phono-Graphix is a multisensory, phonetic approach that is faster-paced than Orton-Gillingham and encourages children to apply concepts quickly to reading real text. The method was developed by Carmen and Geoffrey McGuiness, authors of the book *Reading Reflex*. At the outset, children are taught that letters are pictures of sounds, that some sound pictures have more than one letter, and that some sound pictures represent more than one sound. Starting with eight sound pictures—six consonants and two vowels—the student immediately begins building and reading words. Manipulatives are used in a variety of games and exercises, along with a whiteboard and markers. During writing practice, the child says the sound of each letter as he writes each word.

A key aspect of Phono-Graphix is avoidance of drills. Rather than requiring that the child fully master every letter sound before progressing, the concepts are reinforced through the child's practice and experience with reading words in context, and with immediate correction of errors by the teacher or tutor. Because of its relative simplicity and faster pace, many parents prefer to start with this approach, especially if working on their own with their child.

Emerging Research—Comprehensive Word Study

Some leading dyslexia researchers now advocate programs built upon study of whole words. Students learn to focus on multiple aspects of each word, such as the visual sequence and pattern of letters, common letter patterns signifying word meaning, word definitions and derivations, as well as the letter-sound correspondence and the sounds of the whole words. These programs are designed to help students build strong mental connections that will aid in recognizing and understanding real words in print.

DID YOU KNOW?

One of the most powerful predictors of reading comprehension abilities is the speed and accuracy of reading single words. In addition to being able to quickly recognize words, the students must also know the meaning. Knowledge of word meanings is the most important single factor in reading or listening comprehension.

Dr. Virginia Berninger of the University of Washington has reported impressive gains with a program geared to fifth graders with dyslexia that uses high-interest materials to teach words. Her program uses visual, auditory, and morphological strategies, based on a concept of "triple word form theory." Students focus on learning what each word looks like, what it sounds like, and what it means. According to Dr. Berninger, learning all three elements of the word together builds brain connections that foster a "jump-start" in reading.

Another researcher, Dr. Maryanne Wolf at Tufts University, has developed a program called RAVE-O, which is an acronym for Retrieval, Automaticity, Vocabulary Elaboration, Orthography. RAVE-O is based on the idea that the more a child knows about a word, the faster and better the word is read and understood. This approach teaches core words using a variety of activities and games that emphasize different skills, such as visual recognition of common patterns, or using cards with pictures to depict multiple word meanings. Gamelike activities are used to build speed and accuracy of each underlying skill.

Strategies for Building Fluency and Comprehension
Phonetic approaches will enable a child to learn to read short, easily decodable words, but your child will need to learn additional strategies to recognize longer words and words with irregular spelling patterns. Such words become more common as a child progresses beyond primary level. The older child with dyslexia needs to have workable strategies that are geared to higher reading

levels; otherwise, the child will tend to become bogged down, habitually reading in a slow, labored, and halting manner.

Building Fluency

Once your child is able to recognize words in print, it is crucial that she also gain an ability to read smoothly and at an efficient pace. If she continues to hesitate and stumble during reading, her slow pace undermines comprehension—by the time she gets to the end of a sentence she will have forgotten what was at the beginning. The best way for a child to develop reading fluency is through practice, both through oral and silent reading.

A BETTER PARENTING PRACTICE

Listening to stories read aloud or on tape can help your child build fluency, as it helps the student gain a better sense of the structure and flow of written language and enhances vocabulary.

One approach to building fluency is for the student to repeatedly read the same passage or short story, under the guidance of a tutor, or with a computer or tape recorder, or with peer assistance or a student partner or buddy. Reading can be done in a timed context to build speed, and the teacher, peer, or recording device promotes accuracy. Computer-assisted programs such as *Read Naturally* or *ReadOn* interactive software offer the benefit of instant feedback in a setting that can be controlled by your child.

Alternatively, your child may be encouraged to read along with tape-recorded passages of a book. For example, with the Carbo Recorded-Book Method, the teacher records small segments of a few minutes each of high-interest reading materials onto tape cassettes in short phrases, at a slightly slower speed than normal, to allow the child with reading difficulties to follow along while looking at the same passage in print. The student listens repeatedly to the recording while reading along, later reading the passage unassisted to the teacher.

Visualization and Reading Comprehension

One of the most effective ways to help improve reading comprehension is to encourage your child to form mental pictures of the events described in the stories she reads. This strategy is especially useful for children with dyslexia, who tend to be highly imaginative and visually oriented. Studies consistently show that children who are encouraged to use visual imagery have improved performance on tests of comprehension and recall of materials. Although your child may be a daydreamer who finds mental imagery natural in contexts other than reading, she may struggle to relate the words on the page to mental pictures. When she does try to visualize the story, she may get lost in her thoughts and lose track of the words on the page. She will benefit from a teaching method geared to make sure that she understands and thinks about word meaning as she reads, and provides a specific scheme for visualizing.

Mental imagery can also be promoted through modeling by the teacher and use of open- ended questions during and after reading. It is also useful to integrate the child's own art work with story reading, such as having the child draw a map or diagram of events, or represent the story in cartoon form. However, illustrations embodied in a book's text generally do not promote the formation of a child's own mental images; while richly illustrated text is very appropriate to build interest in young children, studies show that older children report forming fewer, not more, mental images when text is illustrated.

School-Based Programs for Dyslexia

There are a variety of instructional programs geared to teaching struggling readers that are used in public schools and specialized private schools for dyslexia. Many of these are based on Orton-Gillingham principles, but they have been adapted for classroom use and many also incorporate strategies to build reading fluency and comprehension, teach spelling, and develop writing composition skills. Some of the more widely used approaches are:

- **Spalding Method:** Developed by Romalda Spalding, author of *The Writing Road to Reading*, this approach combines phonics instruction with handwriting practice. Students also practice writing composition, beginning with words in spelling notebooks compiled during dictation. The method also emphasizes early exposure to high quality children's literature, which is incorporated into the curriculum through oral reading and discussion.

- **Slingerland Approach:** Developed by Beth Slingerland, a teacher who studied with Samuel Orton, this method has been widely implemented at private schools geared to teaching children with dyslexia. Reading is taught sequentially, proceeding from single letters and symbols to one-syllable words, and then to longer words. Multisensory approaches are emphasized throughout, with each step of instruction incorporating auditory, visual, and kinesthetic channels. Slingerland includes teaching of visual strategies for recognition of phonetically irregular words, and also provides explicit, systematic instruction in the development of vocabulary and reading comprehension.

- **The Herman Method for Reversing Reading Failure:** Named for teacher Renee Herman, this program starts each student at his point of deficit and sequentially teaches mastery of up to twenty skill levels. Students are not given reading material until they have mastered all necessary underlying skills. The program emphasizes visual and tactile exercises to aid in learning the appearance and sound of letters. In addition to decoding, the method also teaches reading strategies for sight words, contextual clues, and dictionary skills, with consistent emphasis on comprehension.

- **Wilson Reading System:** This is a twelve-step program developed especially for older children and teenagers with dyslexia. Wilson includes a unique sound-tapping system to help the student learn to differentiate phonemes, and uses a simplified method of syllable division. It uses extensive, controlled text-reading material to correspond with the skills taught. Concepts are taught with manipulation of cards containing phonemes, syllables, and suffixes. Fluency is emphasized throughout the program. The program also focuses on oral expressive language development through vocabulary instruction, and building comprehension through visualization techniques.

- **REWARDS:** REWARDS is an acronym for Reading Excellence: Word Attack and Rate Development Strategies. Geared to children in fourth through twelfth grades, it consists of twenty classroom lessons, usually given over the course of five weeks. Students are taught to use and combine several alternative strategies to analyze word structure and segment words into parts, including phonetic blending strategies and recognizing affixes, helping them learn a flexible approach aimed at more efficient word recognition.

- **Great Leaps Reading**: This program is designed to be taught in short five- to ten-minute practice sessions, working one-on-one with a teacher or tutor. The goal is to minimize errors in reading through immediate feedback and modeling of the teacher. As soon as the child meets the goal with one passage, he "leaps" to a slightly more difficult level. One unique aspect of the program is that it focuses on teaching sight words via small phrases, such as *"when we try"* or *"who is that,"* with the idea that reading phrases in context will work around the common tendency of struggling readers to skip or stumble over small function words, like "the" or "from."

Intensive Tutoring for Language Processing

Lindamood-Bell Learning Processes is a set of specific programs geared to addressing different types of underlying weaknesses associated with reading difficulties, through a series of programs of intensive therapy and practice. Each program is geared to deal with a different set of language processing issues, and students are evaluated at the outset to determine which services will best meet their current learning needs.

Training usually begins with *Lindamood Phonemic Sequencing* (LIPS), which builds phonemic awareness and decoding skills through developing awareness of the mouth actions which produce speech sounds.

More advanced reading skills are taught with *Seeing Stars: Symbol Imagery for Phonemic Awareness, Sight Words and Spelling,* which develops the ability to mentally visualize the identity, number, and sequence of letters for the sounds within words. A third program, called *Visualizing and Verbalizing*, builds reading comprehension and critical thinking skills by enhancing the child's ability to create mental images related to language and reading, and to describe the images in words. The therapist uses a systematic series of questions such as asking about color, size, shape, or movement to stimulate detailed and vivid imagery.

Lindamood-Bell is very highly regarded but also requires a substantial commitment of time. The recommended intensive format for each program involves one-on-one therapy, four hours a day for four to six weeks. If you work through an authorized Lindamood-Bell learning center, the program can also be very expensive, especially if you need to enroll your child sequentially in two or three separate program series. A modified version of the program may be available through your child's school or a private tutor who has attended a workshop or received related training.

Chapter 6

Specialized Therapies for Dyslexia

Ten Things You Will Learn in This Chapter

- How dyslexia therapy differs from tutoring.
- How to choose a program for your child.
- How exercises to build memory and other cognitive skills such as Audiblox or PACE can help your child learn.
- How auditory integration training programs may help address symptoms of dyslexia.
- How vision training or specialized lenses may help your child become a better reader.
- How programs to improve balance and coordination can build brain function.
- Why one doctor advocates medications to address inner-ear problems.
- How an approach focused on building up strengths rather than remediating weaknesses.
- How All Kinds of Minds provides an alternative system for evaluating and planning for your child's needs.
- How the Davis Dyslexia Correction program combines therapy to address perceptual and attention problem with specific strategies for reading.

How Therapy Differs from Tutoring

A dyslexia therapy is aimed at treating the underlying causes of dyslexia, or addressing specific skill deficits that are seen as precursors to developing the ability to read and write. It differs from tutoring because the goal is to find ways to enhance your child's ability to learn, rather than to directly teach reading. Some therapies are based on novel theories as to the causes of dyslexia, and some are controversial; however, all the therapies profiled in this chapter are now well-established and widely used. These treatments cannot cure dyslexia, but a single program or a combination of approaches may eliminate or minimize many of the symptoms of dyslexia and enable your child to learn more efficiently.

Choosing a Program

In choosing a dyslexia program for your child, it will help to understand the various types of programs. Some programs are geared toward building on your child's academic and intellectual strengths, whereas others are focused mostly on addressing weaknesses. The programs that focus on weaknesses usually offer some sort of skill-building exercises or training. Most do not include specific instruction on reading; these programs are either based on the assumption that acquisition of the underlying skills taught will enable your child to learn to read well on his own, or that the treatment program will be followed by appropriate tutoring.

When considering a program for your child, you should ask what specific problem or symptom will be treated, and what the expected outcome of such treatment will be. You also need to consider whether you will need to supplement the program with additional tutoring or therapies for your child, and if so, what sort of extra support is recommended.

The best place to start learning about a program is by critically reading information available from the program providers, such as in books, brochures, or on their websites. Once you have a basic understanding of what the program claims to offer, you should explore other sources of information, including contacting references.

Beware of Overstated Claims

You should be skeptical of commercial programs that claim to be "scientifically proven" or to "cure" dyslexia—at this time, there is no such thing. At best, there is limited research which provides partial evidence to support various theories and methodologies. Claims about "research" often exaggerate the impact of preliminary studies and surveys, and in many cases the research has been commissioned by individuals with a financial interest in the success of the program.

Programs that address skill areas or abilities other than reading can be very important, and they often fill an important gap that is missed when parents utilize tutoring alone. After all, if your child has a hearing or vision impairment, no amount of teaching is going to succeed when the underlying perceptual barrier stands in the way. However, most alternative therapies address only one cognitive or perceptual area, and they typically do not include specific instruction in reading. Your child will not succeed unless all areas of need are addressed. You will need to carefully evaluate your child's needs and the focus of any treatment program in order to decide which is best for your child.

Cognitive Skill Building

Although dyslexia does not affect intelligence, many children with dyslexia have difficulties with short-term memory, logical reasoning, perceptual discrimination, or other thought processes. Some educators believe that these deficits are at the root of the reading problems associated with dyslexia, and have developed programs aimed at building these underlying skills. The idea is to exercise the brain so as to improve your child's memory, ability to concentrate, and integrate new information, in the same way physical conditioning exercises might be used to build an athlete's strength before practicing his sport.

Audiblox

Audiblox is a system of exercises aimed at the development of foundational learning skills, developed by Dr. Jan Strydom, a South African educator. The goal is to improve cognitive abilities such as concentration, perceptual skills, memory, number concepts, and motor coordination. Although it is possible to hire a therapist to work with your child, Audiblox materials are designed for ease of use and are sold in kit form. The kit contains colored blocks and cards printed with colored patterns, and a book detailing games and practice activities using these materials. The kit also includes a student reading book with a story made up of the most commonly used words in English, and word cards and lists to be learned by memory in conjunction with reading the book. Although geared for all ages, Audiblox can also be started with children as young as age three. The program developers recommend that your school-age child practice the exercises for about three hours a week; you should expect to see improvements within six weeks to three months of sustained practice.

PACE and BrainSkills

Processing and Cognitive Enhancement (PACE) is an intense program of exercises targeted to strengthen weak skills, such as difficulties with memory or processing speed. *BrainSkills* is a simplified version of the PACE program developed for home use. Both programs are done with a parent or tutor working one-on-one with the child, usually for an hour a day over the course of twelve weeks, with sequenced and repetitive activities that become progressively more difficult as the child's skill level increases. The program can address skills such as processing speed, working memory, visual processing, auditory analysis, and logical reasoning. A related program called *Master the Code* is specifically geared toward reading skills.

Auditory Training Therapies

Some researchers believe that dyslexia is caused by difficulties in hearing and distinguishing sounds at different frequencies, in perceiving rhythms, or in coordinating sounds heard with each ear. If children with dyslexia typically have difficulty sorting out the sounds of language, perhaps the root of the problem is that they have difficulty recognizing or filtering all types of sounds. There are now a variety of programs to train the child to be a better listener, based on the idea that fixing the underlying perceptual barrier will resolve the dyslexia as well.

Berard Auditory Integration Training

The goal of Berard Auditory Integration Training (AIT) is to help your child overcome hypersensitivity or difficulty hearing sound at certain pitches and frequencies through listening practice geared to building his tolerance to sounds and listening acuity. The program can help children who have attention deficit disorder, autism, or central auditory processing disorder, as well as dyslexia.

DOES THIS SOUND LIKE YOUR CHILD?

Your child may benefit from an auditory training program if he appears to have difficulty listening or following directions, if he seems to have a tendency to zone out or daydream, or if he is unusually sensitive to or distraught by loud noises or sounds within certain frequencies.

Dr. Guy Berard, the developer of AIT, believes that auditory processing problems are caused by hypersensitive hearing. He developed an electronic device called an AudioKinetron that randomizes and filters music frequencies. The theory behind the program is that the tiny acoustic reflex muscle in the inner ear can be exercised by listening to varying pitches and frequencies, and that such exercise will reduce pain or sensitivity to loud noises or certain frequencies, and stimulate the mental pathways that transmit and respond to sound. Your child listens to electronically altered pop music over the course of twenty half-hour sessions for ten consecutive days. At the end of the training, your child's hearing should show significant improvement with most frequencies being perceived within normal ranges. This should be reflected in behavioral changes, some of which may be observed immediately. Other changes will become evident over a period of three to six months following treatment, as your child's overall functioning improves as a response to his improved hearing ability.

The Tomatis Method

In the 1950s, Dr. Alfred Tomatis found that many children with learning disabilities have difficulty hearing high sound frequencies, as well as with distinguishing between low- and high-pitched sound frequencies. He theorized that language problems could be caused by an inefficient pattern of dominance. Sounds captured by the right ear are directly transmitted to the language center in the left brain. On the other hand, sounds captured by the left ear go first to the right brain before being transmitted to the language center in the left brain, which is a less efficient route for listening to the sounds of language. Thus an imbalance in the hearing process could result in difficulties in making sense of language.

Dr. Tomatis developed a listening device to retrain the ear by switching constantly between two channels, one emphasizing low-pitched sounds, and the other accentuating higher frequencies. The switching forces the ear to adjust continually to changing sounds. Your child listens to electronically filtered recordings of Mozart, his mother's voice, and Gregorian chants through headphones that have a special bone conductor on the top. The listening exercises are gradually combined with active exercising using the voice to maintain learning.

DID YOU KNOW?

Research shows that children with dyslexia have difficulty detecting beats in sounds with a strong rhythm. Awareness of beats may influence the way young children assimilate speech patterns and affect their ability to break down the sounds of words. One dyslexia researcher has found that classroom music lessons help build phonologic and spelling skills.

Interactive Metronome

Interactive Metronome (IM) uses special interactive equipment in order to improve your child's sense of rhythm and timing. With this program, your child performs repetitive hand or foot exercises in time with a computer-generated beat; he wears headsets to listen to guide tones, and sensors attached to his hand or foot send signals back to the computer. If your child hits ahead of the beat, he hears an auditory guide tone in the left side of his head; if he hits after the beat, the tone comes from the right. When your child is able to hit on the beat, a reward tone is heard simultaneously through both ears. The computer records reaction time in milliseconds and provides a score; the goal is to reduce the time interval to optimum levels.

By learning to keep the beat, your child becomes more able to sustain focus, disregard distractions, and stay on task for longer periods of time. This program is done under the guidance of a specially trained therapist, and takes about three to five weeks to complete, with three to five hour-long sessions each week.

Programs that Address Vision

Many vision care professionals believe that reading problems associated with dyslexia can be caused by underlying vision deficits, such as problems with visual tracking or unusual sensitivity to light or glare. Even if such problems are not the cause of dyslexia, they often aggravate the symptoms, and therapies which address vision problems often seem to result in significant improvement in reading skills.

Vision Therapy

Vision impairments can affect the way that your child focuses on print and her ability to shift focus from one word to the next. These problems can cause blurred vision, eyestrain, headaches, and double vision when reading. Your child may frequently lose his place, omit words, close one eye, or show difficulty sustaining reading for long. It is very possible for your child to have 20/20 vision but still have undetected vision problems that impact her ability to read.

These problems are correctable, sometimes with specialized lenses or prisms, or with specific exercises and practice geared to help your child learn to use his eyes effectively. Some of the visual skills that may affect reading are the ability to quickly locate and inspect a series of stationary objects, such as moving from word to word while reading (fixation); the ability to clearly see and understand objects at near distances, such as print on a page (near vision acuity); the ability to shift focus from near to far quickly, such as looking from a chalkboard to a book (accommodation); and the ability to keep both eyes aligned on a book while reading (binocularity). Different approaches and exercises are tailored to various problems; for example, your child may practice shifting focus from a near to far object and back with one eye covered, and then repeat the exercise with the other eye covered.

A developmental optometrist will develop an individualized program for your child; treatment may be from several weeks to several months depending upon the condition. Some insurance plans may cover vision training.

Irlen Lenses

Psychologist Helen Irlen, author of the book *Reading by the Colors*, found that many children she worked with were able to improve reading fluency when using colored lenses. She coined the term Scotopic Sensitivity Syndrome, or Irlen Syndrome, to describe the condition that her approach proved effective in treating. Some symptoms of Irlen Syndrome are discomfort working under bright lights or fluorescent lights, problems with reading print on white or high gloss paper, or perceiving print as shifting or blurring.

If you choose to have your child evaluated at an Irlen Center, your child will first be screened to determine whether reading improves with use of a colored overlay; if this seems to help, your child will work with a diagnostician using a wide array of colored lenses to determine the precise color that seems to work best for your child. You can also achieve some of the benefits of this approach by buying colored overlays for your child to use from an art or theatrical supply store. Although this is not as precise as having your child evaluated at an Irlen Center, it may afford similar relief.

Balance and Coordination

Some researchers believe that dyslexia stems from difficulties with physical coordination or balance. Many children with dyslexia do have difficulty acquiring physical skills, such as learning to tie their shoes or ride a bicycle, or may seem clumsy and accident-prone; however, these symptoms are not universal. Various theories have been proposed as to the underlying reasons for such difficulties, but treatment is generally geared toward specific exercises to build the skills thought to be missing.

Brain Gym

Brain Gym is a series of twenty-six exercises designed to help learners coordinate their brains and their bodies better. It consists of simple movements similar to the natural movements, such as crawling, that are part of early childhood development. The goal of the program is to improve your child's sense of balance and ability to focus, as well as to relieve stress. Many of the movements can be done while a child is seated, and the exercises can be easily incorporated into a classroom setting. This approach is intended to enhance the learning process for all children, but it can be very helpful to children with attention-focus problems and learning disabilities. This program will not resolve all problems, but it is a simple and easy-to-learn approach that may provide a needed boost to your child's overall readiness to learn.

Balance Training

Balametrics, or *Learning Breakthrough*, is a system of balance training exercises geared to improving both small and large motor coordination, balance, and cross-lateral movements. Your child could work with a therapist trained in this approach, or you can purchase a home kit which includes a special balance board set on rockers called a Belgau Balance Board, as well as bean bags and other tools to use in conjunction with the training.

A similar approach called *Dore* was established in the United Kingdom in 2002, and was based on a theory that dyslexia stems from a delay in development of the cerebellum, an area at the base of the brain that is important to developing physical coordination and automatic motor skills. The program combined at-home exercises with regular visits to the Dore center for assessments and training with new exercises. The program was controversial because of aggressive marketing practices and claims by its developer that it offered a "miracle cure." The program was promoted by a millionaire businessman, Wynford Dore, who rapidly opened centers throughout the world. In 2008, most Dore centers in the United States, United Kingdom, and Australia were shut down because of financial difficulties, though at least one U.S.–based center not directly affiliated with the Dore company continued to offer the program under a pre-existing licensing agreement.

Levinson Medical Center

Dr. Harold Levinson is a psychiatrist and the author of several books about dyslexia, including *Smart but Feeling Dumb* and *The Upside-Down Kids*. Dr. Levinson believes that dyslexia stems from a disturbance in the inner ear, which is critical for maintaining balance; he theorizes that this disturbance causes the brain to receive scrambled signals, which in turn produces the symptoms commonly associated with dyslexia. Dr. Levinson treats patients with a combination of medications, using antimotion sickness antihistamines and stimulants such as Ritalin, which is commonly used to regulate attention focus.

Although Dr. Levinson has published a number of books describing his approach, his theories are unorthodox and have not been generally accepted by other medical professionals. Most educators and therapists do not feel that prescription medications should be used to treat dyslexia, and these medications can produce unwanted side effects.

Comprehensive and Integrated Approaches

An alternative way of addressing your child's needs is to seek a comprehensive approach, based on looking at all factors impacting learning together, and building largely upon your child's strengths rather than simply trying to remediate separate areas of weakness. Such an approach can be more enjoyable for your child and build confidence and self-esteem, and also can result in greater success over the long run.

All Kinds of Minds

All Kinds of Minds helps children achieve success through diagnostic services and guidance. Pioneered by Dr. Mel Levine, this is not a specific treatment method, but a framework for planning interventions based on understanding your child's learning process, with an emphasis on identifying your child's specific areas of strength. The approach begins with an in-depth evaluation at a Student Success Center, focusing on factors that influence the learning process, such as attention, memory, language, and cognition. Standardized IQ or achievement tests are not used, and labels such as "learning disabled" or "dyslexia" are avoided; instead, the goal is to provide a complete picture of your child's unique pattern of learning.

Your child will also be involved in a dynamic process called *demystification*, where your child works with a therapist to gain a better understanding of her own learning needs. This process helps your child gain insight and learn the language needed to chart her own learning path and interact more successfully with teachers. Working with you and your child, the clinicians help develop a learning plan that includes accommodations (or "bypass strategies") to work around weaknesses; specific interventions that are targeted at areas causing breakdowns in the learning process; strategies to enhance inherent strengths; and "affinity development," a process to help your child recognize and deepen areas of high interest.

In the end, you will have an action plan geared to making your child a successful and empowered learner, rather than aimed merely at helping him overcome weaknesses. Because of his own role in the process, your child will have a sense of control and an increased level of confidence and motivation. However, this approach gives you a roadmap, but does not implement the specific steps. Your child will have support that will help forge a path to success, but a good deal of responsibility for arranging and negotiating interventions and modifications remains on your shoulders.

Davis Dyslexia Correction

Davis Dyslexia Correction is a comprehensive approach geared to the creative thinking strengths that accompany dyslexia. It combines techniques to resolve attention-focusing issues and perceptual problems with hands-on methods for mastering sight words and improving reading fluency. For children age eight and above, it begins with a one-week intensive program of individual counseling that breaks down major learning barriers and often results in dramatic reading improvement. This is followed with implementation and practice of the Davis methods at home, mostly through a systematic program of clay modeling, which generally takes between six and eighteen months to complete.

Description of Program

Ronald Dell Davis, author of the book *The Gift of Dyslexia*, developed the program in part based on his own experiences. Davis theorized that people with dyslexia think mainly in pictures or sensory impressions, and experience confusion in sorting out the meaning of printed words and symbols. The confusion results in a state of disorientation, which in turn leads to misperceptions typically associated with dyslexia, such as the sense that letters on a page are moving, or confusion of the sequence and appearance of letters and numerals.

The Davis program begins with "Orientation Counseling," a type of mental training that will help your child recognize and eliminate visual perceptual distortions, such as letter transpositions or the false sense that letters are shifting position, as well as to resolve auditory perceptual confusion. Your child will also learn specific self-help strategies to regulate her energy level, and practice tossing Koosh balls to improve balance and physical coordination.

The Davis program also includes and emphasizes strategies for building reading fluency and comprehension.

The primary strategy, "Davis Symbol Mastery," is based on the idea that a child with dyslexia needs to create mental pictures for words before he can read or understand words in print. While your child probably understands nouns such as "dog" or "lion," he may stumble over words like "for" or "in" because he has no clear mental image to go along with the word. The focus of the Davis program is to help the child supply his own pictures for each word.

The primary tools of the Davis program are a dictionary and clay. Your child learns how to look up words, how to use the pronunciation key to find out how each word sounds, and how to use the definition and example sentences as a starting point for mastering the meaning of the word. Your child will then use clay to form the letters of each word, and also make a three-dimensional model to depict the word's meaning. The child will model small, abstract words such as *the* or *and*, and may also use this approach to understand larger words or concepts such as *sequence* or *time*. Reading practice also includes a technique called "Spell Reading," which builds visual tracking, sequencing, and whole word recognition skills, and "Picture-at-Punctuation," an approach incorporating visualization to build comprehension skills.

DOES THIS SOUND LIKE YOUR CHILD?

Davis providers can work with almost any child who has symptoms of dyslexia, but the program is particularly appropriate for children who have difficulty gaining reading fluency, have difficulties with letter reversals and transpositions, or tend to stumble over or omit small words when reading.

Davis Program Outcomes

The Davis program successfully combines highly targeted techniques for resolving various perceptual issues with specific strategies to develop reading skills. These include addressing distortions of visual perception and hearing, building visual tracking skills, developing an understanding of concepts such as sequence and order, learning specific tools to help focus and sustain attention and self-monitor energy levels, and using reading strategies geared to developing fluency and strong comprehension skills.

Because of its integrated approach, combining correction of underlying perceptual problems with targeted therapy to find and eliminate each child's individual learning blocks, or *triggers*, the program often produces very rapid reading gains. With older children and teenagers, it is common for word recognition and reading fluency skills to jump by three to five grade levels during the initial week. However, the Davis techniques must be practiced after the program in order for progress to continue and initial gains to be sustained.

Students who complete the Davis program often gain proficiency at or above grade level and may become very capable and enthusiastic readers. However, because the program does not encourage phonetic decoding strategies, it remains controversial among many educators who prefer traditional tutoring. The program is generally not appropriate for children relying on medications such as Ritalin to regulate attention level or behavior, as such medications impede the ability to reliably learn the various mental self-regulation techniques. The program is most likely to be successful if your child is motivated to follow through with using the techniques on his own.

Chapter 7

Strategies to Help Your Child at Home

Ten Things You Will Learn in This Chapter

- How to help your child develop prereading skills.

- Some strategies to help your child learn early reading skills.

- What you can do to build reading fluency and make reading more enjoyable.

- Tips and strategies for tutoring or building basic reading skills.

- How you can help your child improve spelling by building visual memory.

- Tips for studying common word patterns to improve spelling skills.

- How you can encourage your child to write stories and poems.

- Strategies to help your child get started and organize her ideas for writing.

- Ways to help your child better understand math concepts.

- How to help your child with math word problems.

Teaching Prereading Skills

You may be able to help your child avoid many difficulties typically associated with dyslexia if you can reach your child in the preschool years and help develop foundational skills. These skills are vital to reading acquisition, but may be harder to acquire as the child grows older.

If your child is not yet reading, you can help him focus on the sounds of words through nursery rhymes and song lyrics. Introduce your child to the idea of rhyming, and encourage him in playful conversation to make up his own rhymes. Sing songs like "Down by the Bay" ("Did you ever see a moose / Kissing a goose?") and help your child invent his own lyrics. Help your child focus on smaller word segments and phonemes by playing games with the sounds of the words; teach songs like "Apples and Bananas" ("I like to eat, eat, eat, eat / apples and bananas / I like to ate, ate, ate, ate / ay-ples and bay-nay-nays").

Include songs and games that involve clapping, jumping, and other movements to music. This will help your child develop a stronger sense of the rhythm of language and may help with skills related to right/left bodily coordination or timing that are implicated in dyslexia.

A BETTER PARENTING PRACTICE

Encourage games and activities that involve sorting and organizing items, as well as practice with order and sequence. Help your child develop an awareness of temporal sequence (beginning/middle/end), as well as spatial relationships (above/below, order/under, in/out, left/right). Your child can explore these concepts while playing with blocks, putting away toys, or helping to set the table.

When your child is very young, gently introduce the habit of visually scanning or counting objects from left to right. For example, you might line up a row of toys and hold his hand to count each one, beginning with the left side and moving toward the right. You can begin this even before the child knows the difference between left and right; the idea is to try to create a habit of always beginning from the left and moving to the right, in the hope that will make the transition to reading easier.

Learning Letters

Introduce your child to letters by teaching both the sound and the name of each letter. The letters do not need to be taught in order, but it is important that a young child associates a letter such as K with both its sound (kuh) and its name ("kay"). You may want to start by helping your child learn the letters in his own name, and then move on to names of other family members. Show your child how each letter relates to the sounds in the name, but do not try to drill or teach a very young child to apply that information in other contexts. For example, you might point to each letter in the name Kevin and say the sound; you might even show your child how that name contains the word "in" and later remind him of that pattern when showing him rhyming words like "bin" or "tin." With a very young child, keep these "lessons" casual, as things that you mention when the occasion arises. You want your child to start to understand the idea that letters represent sounds, and that words are composed by combining the sounds in an orderly way; formal instruction can wait until your child starts school.

Draw your child's attention to different letters on signs and in print, such as words on the front of cereal boxes. Encourage him to make his own letters by molding them with clay or Play-Doh, and supply toys such as magnetic letters that allow him to move and touch the letters.

Never push your young child to learn something he seems to have difficulty with. It is cute when a preschooler has learned to sing his ABCs, but if he doesn't have a clue as to what each letter looks like or that letters represent sounds, it is not going to help him read. Once frustration sets in, your child is not likely to learn from the experience.

Supporting the School-Age Reader

Most children with dyslexia experience great difficulty learning to read at school. Even after your child has mastered the basics, he may read slowly and laboriously, with considerable effort. If your child is receiving intensive remedial instruction at school, you should focus efforts at home on making reading a fun and pleasurable activity—this will help build and sustain motivation and build a familiarity with literature that will support development of advanced comprehension skills.

Reading with Your Child

Continue to read aloud to your child at home. When reading for pleasure, allow your struggling reader to relax and listen attentively without being expected to read. You should still encourage your child to sit next to you, so he can see the pages of the book as you read. If you are helping your child with a book that must be read for school, encourage your child to participate by taking turns reading; you can ask your child to read a sentence or a paragraph, then read several paragraphs yourself, and then let your child have another turn.

In books with a lot of dialogue, another technique for shared reading is to let your child take the role of one (or more) of the characters, reading the quoted words for that character. This is also a good opportunity to help your child focus on punctuation, such as quotation marks, commas, periods, exclamation points, and question marks. Many children with dyslexia do not understand what punctuation means, and they tend to ignore or disregard punctuation marks when reading because they are so focused on trying to decipher the letters and words. With oral reading, punctuation takes on added significance, as it provides information about when the reader should pause, and the intonation that should be used.

When your child is reading aloud, do not interrupt to correct mistakes that do not change meaning, such as reading "mom" for "mother." Frequent interruptions will cause your child to lose confidence and make comprehension more difficult. If your child stumbles over a word, simply tell her what it is. Do not try to use teaching techniques, such as having her sound out words, at this time. Instead, enjoy the story together, discuss the plot, praise your child for her efforts when she reads aloud and is able to figure out some words on her own.

Teaching Reading Skills

If you are working with your child to try to teach reading or supplement instruction at school, do the "lessons" at a separate time—and with different books—than reading for pleasure or to gain experience. Oral and shared reading should be used to build fluency and comprehension skills, as well as to instill a love of literature and build motivation for reading.

If your child is in school but is not receiving specialized reading instruction, or if you are not happy with the methods being used, you may choose to tutor your child on your own. Make sure that your child wants to learn from you; if your child feels overwhelmed and exhausted from his efforts each day at school, he may need your loving support and a chance to relax far more than he needs more lessons.

If you are teaching your child on your own, you may want to use some of the methods and techniques profiled in Chapters 5 and 6, using books or kits developed for home use. Try to choose a single method, starting with one that seems comfortable for you and easy to implement; mixing more than one approach at the beginning can simply cause greater confusion. If your child does not seem to be making progress after several weeks, or seems to reach a plateau or barrier after several months, you can then consider moving on to a different method.

If your child is in school and you are teaching at home using different techniques, explain to your child that there is more than one way to figure out words. Point out that you are going to teach or practice a different strategy than the one his teacher uses. Explain that he should use the time with you to practice the new strategy, but that when he reads on his own he should use whichever is easiest for him.

If your child has difficulty with sounding out by sequentially blending separate word sounds, such as putting the sounds of /b/, /a/, and /t/ together to make "bat," you might try an alternate approach of teaching onset and rime (see the article by Stephanie Smith at *www.crossboweducation.com/*). This involves focusing attention on the beginning sound (onset) of a word or syllable, and then teaching the remaining single-syllable sound combination (rime) as a whole. For example, in the word "bat" the onset is /b/, while the rime is "at." Knowing the "at" rime will make it easier for your child to learn cat, hat, rat, and so on.

DID YOU KNOW?

Your child may find it helpful to hold an index card or ruler under each line of text as he reads. This will help him stay focused on the text. It is also possible to purchase a reading guide with a colored filter in

the center, which is designed so that your child can
move it down the page as he reads.

Observe your child to see what sort of words gives
him the most trouble, and to see what sort of strategies he typically uses for decoding. Use common sense
so that you can make practical suggestions, geared to
the types of problems he is having, and the type of
words he is trying to read. Keep in mind that once your
child is able to read at first or second grade level, he
will encounter more words that are phonetically irregular, and will need to learn other skills beyond simply
phonetic decoding to progress. You may be able to
help him improve reading skills by learning to look for
familiar letter patterns, to break words down into syllables or word segments, or to recognize common roots
and affixes. Teach him to look at the whole word before
starting to decode; he may recognize a familiar pattern
or segment toward the end of the word that will make
word recognition easier.

Helping with Spelling

Difficulty with spelling is the most common and persistent difficulty that accompanies dyslexia. Even after
your child becomes a capable reader, his writing is
likely to be riddled with spelling errors. One reason is
the extreme variability of English spelling; almost every
"rule" that can be taught has numerous exceptions,
and many words simply are not spelled the way they
sound.

Building Visual Memory for Spelling

Good spellers generally have strong visual memories for what words look like in print. Try to avoid study or practice techniques that expose your child to incorrectly spelled versions of the word. Many children with dyslexia have strong visual memories, but they will remember erroneous spellings as easily as correct ones, and they will have no way to remember which is right. Teachers might try to make spelling homework fun by offering a practice quiz where your child must select the correct word from a list of incorrect spellings, or find the word in a puzzle where the letters are scrambled. Your child may enjoy some of these games, but they are counterproductive for learning correct spelling.

A BETTER PARENTING PRACTICE

When practicing spelling words at home, observe your child to see whether she does better when asked to orally spell the words as opposed to writing them. This will give you a clue as to how to best reach your child. If your child does better with oral spelling, encourage her to say the letters out loud as she practices writing her spelling words.

One technique that sometimes works for children with dyslexia is to learn how to spell a word backwards as well as forward. Encourage your child to try to visualize the word in his mind; with a clear mental picture, the word can be spelled backwards by "seeing" the letters in order and calling off the letters from right to left.

Word Families and Patterns

Good spellers also recognize familiar spelling patterns and understand morphological word structure, including common prefixes, roots, and suffixes. It will be easier for your child to learn when words are taught in groups that share a common pattern or structure. This is better than learning "rules" in isolation, especially with rules that have many exceptions. A popular program for home use which builds on common word elements is AVKO Sequential Spelling, which was developed specifically for children with dyslexia. Make sure that your child's word list for each study session includes only words reflecting the pattern being studied. Work with your child's teacher to modify school spelling lists so as to avoid confusion, and limit the number of words being studied.

Do not try to teach your child homophones, such as "their" and "there," in the same session. Most people with dyslexia find homophones extremely confusing, and they will not be able to simply memorize the difference. It is better if the words are taught separately with words sharing a similar pattern; for example, "there" can be taught along with "here" and "where." Make sure your child learns word meanings along with spelling; it will aid in memory to associate meanings with spelling patterns, as opposed to individual words. That is, it may be easier to remember that the "ere" sequence is associated with words signifying place ("here, there, everywhere").

Have your child look up words with irregular patterns in the dictionary, to learn about the word derivations and etymology. She will soon discover other keys to spelling—for example, that the word "their" comes from the Old Norse *theirra*. Knowing that some words with similar sounds come from different languages will help your child understand why they are spelled so differently.

Tips for the Reluctant Writer

The best way to help your child become a better writer is to separate the mechanics of writing (spelling, handwriting, punctuation, grammar) from the creative aspects. Your child's strength is in his vivid imagination, a valuable asset in a writer. Help your child learn that writing is a two-stage process; the first stage is getting the ideas on paper; correcting or editing work is the second step.

A BETTER PARENTING PRACTICE

Your child may enjoy reading books written by children's authors who also have dyslexia, such as Patricia Polacco's many richly illustrated story books, including *Thank You Mr. Falker,* where she describes her own early struggles with reading; or Jeanne Betancourt's novel for young readers about a boy with dyslexia, *My Name Is Brain Brian.*

For writing the first draft of an essay or story, follow this rule: there will be no corrections or criticism for spelling or grammar. Your child should be encouraged to write things down in whatever form or order she is comfortable with. Once the ideas are in written form, you can guide your child to developing a more polished version. When your child is very young, you will give a lot of help; as she grows older, she will learn to do more for herself. Remind your child that even professional writers rely on editors to proofread and correct their work.

Mind Mapping

One good technique for getting ideas to flow is mind mapping. To do this, your child starts with a main subject, and writes down a few words or draws a picture representing the idea in the middle of a blank sheet of paper. He should then draw lines or branches radiating out from the center for each main idea he has about the subject; with each line he should write a few words or draw another picture. He can add details to each idea by again writing a few words, connecting them via a line or branch to the idea they relate to.

Once the ideas are written down in a mind map format, you can help your child develop them into written sentences, using the map as a guideline for developing the structure of his paragraph or essay.

Experiment with Different Formats

If your child seems to balk at writing anything in narrative format, have him try writing poetry or verse. Introduce your child to the concept of free verse—poetry that does not have a particular rhythm or cadence, and does not have to rhyme. One of the advantages of writing poetry is that it frees the child from writing conventions, such as the need to use complete sentences. It also allows your child to experiment with the sounds of words and to use novel words that evoke a particular mood or feeling.

Your child might enjoy writing haiku, in part because it is short. Haiku traditionally has three lines consisting of seventeen syllables in total, usually arranged in lines of five, seven, and five syllables. Although the form is very brief, writing haiku will help your child develop sensitivity to the phonetic structure of word segments.

You might also encourage your child to write a play; it is sometimes easier for the budding writer to focus only on the dialogue among the characters. Your child might enjoy presenting her play as a puppet show, or using a video camera to make her own movie using her own written screenplay.

Use Artwork as Inspiration

Your child may do better with writing if you encourage him to draw a picture of his ideas or a story he wants to write, and then use words to describe what is going on in the picture. He might want to write in comic-book or storyboard format, with a series of pictures and a short sentence describing each one. Alternatively, your child might draw a larger, more complex picture, and then write several sentences or paragraphs describing what is going on in the picture. You might also want to encourage your child to write a story, a set of impressions, or a poem about an illustration or artwork in a book.

You will find an intriguing set of pictures to use as writing prompts in *The Mysteries of Harris Burdick*, by Chris Van Allsburg. The book's premise is that the pictures were drawn by a man who disappeared before he could explain what the pictures were about, leaving it up to the reader's imagination to find the story behind each.

Helping with Arithmetic

Most children with dyslexia are ready to understand math concepts, but they often struggle with pencil-and-paper math as it is taught in school. The problem generally stems from difficulty understanding and manipulating math symbols, including numerals as well as symbols for operations, and with difficulty understanding and applying words commonly used to express mathematical concepts. Thus, the language-based disability that is part of dyslexia becomes a liability for learning arithmetic.

Modeling Math Concepts

When your child asks for help with arithmetic, start by finding out whether he understands the concepts underlying the problems he is working on. A child with dyslexia often has unexpected gaps in learning, and so sometimes even a very simple concept may be at the heart of a misunderstanding. Use three-dimensional objects to model mathematical concepts. You might use beans, coins, or small blocks to model functions such as addition, subtraction, and multiplication; you might demonstrate the concept of fractions by measuring liquid in a cup, or by cutting a slice of bread into halves or quarters. Place value can be demonstrated with pennies and dimes. If your child understands the relative value of coins, they can also be used to model fractions or equivalencies.

Many arithmetic or algebraic concepts can also be modeled using geometrical shapes, and a set of pattern blocks can be useful to help your child visualize numerical relationships, such as understanding multiplication, division, and fractions. For example, your child can discover that a rectangle constructed of square blocks that is 3 blocks high and 4 blocks wide will have 12 blocks in all—the same as the problem 3 x 4 = 12.

Explain Words and Symbols

Make sure that your child understands all the symbols used in arithmetic problems, as well as understanding numerals and what they mean. While your child may understand isolated numerals, he may be confused by two-digit numbers, the meaning of 0 (zero), negative numbers, decimals, or commas used in numbers with four or more figures.

Be sure that your child understands all the words used in describing a problem. Your child may be confused by specific terminology—words such as "sum," or "reciprocal," and he may be equally confused by words that are used outside of mathematics, such as "positive" or "even," as well as words signifying relationships such as "from" or "than."

A BETTER PARENTING PRACTICE

Try to avoid situations where your child must copy problems from a book, as children with dyslexia commonly make transposition errors. If your child must copy, encourage her to vocalize the numbers as she writes them—she is less likely to transpose 346 if she says "three, four, six" or "three hundred forty-six" as she writes the numbers. Your child may prefer to have you dictate the problems to her to write down, rather than trying to copy them on her own.

When your child writes out a mathematical problem, use paper with a grid or graph paper to help her keep the numbers lined up properly. If your child is working from a printed sheet of problems, have her circle operational signs such as (+) or (−) in different colors, so that she understands what is expected with each problem. Check to make sure she has copied correctly before she begins to work the problems.

Use Multiple Approaches

Most mathematical problems can be solved in more than one way; the more complex the math, the more likely it is that there are multiple strategies that can be applied. Often, the conventional algorithms taught in school cause unnecessary confusion. For example, your child may be stymied by the concept of "borrowing" or "regrouping" to subtract 6 from 12 on paper, but might be able to solve the same problem quickly in his head, simply by recognizing that 6 is half of 12. Many very complex arithmetic problems can be solved more efficiently by factoring or manipulating the numbers.

Encourage your child to use his knowledge of number concepts to find different approaches for calculation. Although these skills may lead your child to deviate from the approaches taught in the early years, they are the foundations of understanding algebra and higher mathematical concepts. In the long run, your child will do better in math if he is able to turn a problem on its head, or restructure the problem to make it easier, such as restating the problem 15 x 9 as [(15 x 10) – 15] because it is easier to subtract 15 from 150 than to do double-digit multiplication.

Handling Word Problems

Word or story problems are very difficult for children with dyslexia, even when they have a strong understanding of math concepts. To start with, the problem requires reading, which is an effort for your child. Word problems also require highly accurate reading; a missed or misunderstood word can change the entire meaning of the problem. Many of the words used in story problems are also confusing; your child may understand how to "subtract" but be confused by the use of words like "less" or "from" to describe the same concept. Your child may also be confused by the use of pronouns in a story problem—the question "how many of them did he have left?" may leave your child scratching his head wondering what "them" refers to and who "he" is. Finally, your child may be confused by extraneous information in the problem used to describe the setting—the problem may be asking for a calculation of the amount of change to be given for buying movie tickets, but your child is trying to guess from the illustration in the book what movie was playing.

Help your child visualize each problem by imagining or acting out the scenario depicted.

Explain that an arithmetic problem is a puzzle that always requires her to figure out a piece of missing information. Have your child read through the problem—or read it to her—and then ask her if she knows what information the problem calls for her to figure out. (For example, the number of cookies that each child will get.) Then ask your child what information she will need to figure out the answer; guide her, as needed, to look for that specific information in the problem (the total number of cookies and the total number of children). Allow your child to explore the possible ways that she can figure out the answer; there may be more than one acceptable strategy.

Chapter 8

Managing the Homework Load

Ten Things You Will Learn in This Chapter

- How to manage study time.
- Prioritizing assignments for efficiency.
- How to work effectively with your child.
- Study partners and help from other children.
- How computers and word-processing software can help.
- Specialized software to read text to your child.
- Using books on tape and videos.
- Drawing the line to avoid cheating and plagiarism.
- Working with your child's teacher to arrange fair modifications.
- Why it is also important for your child to get adequate rest.

Taming the Homework Dragon

Homework can often become a family battleground, with your child's efforts to complete even routine assignments regularly leading to hours of frustration that invariably end in tears or tantrums. When you try to help your child, you may find that you simply end up arguing, resorting to threats and punishment out of your own frustration. Home life is disrupted as your child's homework demands keep him up well past his expected bedtime, and take away time that you can relax with your spouse and your other children.

There is only one solution: Don't let homework manage you. You need to set limits, and stick to them, both with your child and with the teacher. The purpose of homework is to help your child learn; if it is not fulfilling that purpose, then it simply is not worth the stress that it can cause.

Setting Limits on Study Time

Ask your child's teacher how long she expects her students to spend on homework each night. One good rule of thumb is ten minutes for every grade in school—so a fourth grader may have forty minutes of homework, a sixth grader an hour. Your own child's teacher may expect something more or less. If the teacher gives you a time range that you feel is reasonable—tell her how much time your child is actually spending. The teacher may be stunned to learn that a routine assignment that she expected would take twenty minutes actually takes three hours to complete at your home.

Ask for Modifications

Explain what aspects of the assignments cause difficulty for your child, and ask if the assignments can be modified to better meet your child's abilities and eliminate sticking points. For example, some teachers may insist that children copy out the questions in a book as well as writing the answers. A modification to allow your child to write only the answers may immediately cut homework time in half.

An easy timesaver is simply to reduce the number or length of assignments. If there are thirty multiplication problems on the page, perhaps your child can do ten. If the teacher wants a five paragraph essay, perhaps your child can write two paragraphs.

Set a Time Limit

Whatever modifications you can agree on, also include a time limit. Tell the teacher that you will monitor your child to make sure he puts in effort on homework, and if he is unable to complete the assignment, you will send a note indicating how much time was spent. Ask the teacher to accept partially completed homework if a minimum agreed time has been spent; to give your child credit for doing his homework; and to at least give your child a passing grade.

At home, make sure that your child has a place to do his homework that is free of distractions and where all materials he needs (pens, pencils, paper) are at hand. This should also be a place where you can observe and monitor your child to make sure he is focused on homework. If he is working with a computer, make sure you can see the screen; otherwise, you may find that your son has achieved record high scores with Tetris but failed to even open the word-processing program.

Reach an agreement with your child about the total time to be spent on homework, including the time he will start, and the time he must finish. Use a kitchen timer to keep track of how long your child has been working. If your child has a hard time sustaining attention or sitting still, break up the session with opportunities to relax, stretch, and move around; stop and restart the timer as needed to keep track of actual time worked.

When your child has worked for the requisite time, tell him that his time is up and you are ready to write the note to the teacher. If your child wants to continue working, and he seems to be working at a good pace without frustration, allow him to do so—but remind him that he is allowed to quit at any time. However, do not allow your young child to work beyond the hour that is your family deadline for completing homework, usually the time when your child must start getting ready for bed. Give your child a warning about ten minutes before that time, and suggest that he set his alarm early to complete work in the morning if he protests. Your child's bedtime should be age-appropriate, but it should also be firm.

DID YOU KNOW?

Sleep is essential to learning. During sleep, information and experiences learned during the day become integrated into long-term memory. Thus, it is counterproductive for a child to forego sleep in order to study; he may finish the assignment, but he will weaken his ability to remember and understand the content. Rest is particularly important to children with dyslexia, as their performance deteriorates markedly under conditions of stress or fatigue.

There is one exception to the bedtime rule: If your child ever becomes actively engaged in a task that has always been difficult for him, don't fight success. There may come a time when something seems to click for your child, and for the first time in his life he becomes absorbed in reading a book, or excited about a poem or a story he is writing. If and when this happens, rejoice. Thomas Edison said, "Genius is 1 percent inspiration and 99 percent perspiration"—don't get in the way of the inspiration when you see it. You can reinstate the rules later on.

Setting Priorities for Schoolwork

Help your child learn to set priorities for his schoolwork. Some of your child's homework is probably easy for her; some is quite difficult. Some requires her to do things that she doesn't enjoy, but some tasks might be fun. Some of the homework is important to help your child master a particular skill or learn required material; some is mere busy work, assigned mostly for the sake of having the child do something.

Your job is to help your child learn to sort her work so that homework can be completed in the most efficient manner possible. When your child is very young, this may mean that you make the decisions for her; as she grows older, she will better be able to make these choices on her own.

Encourage your child to complete all assignments that are easy or fun, whether or not they seem useful. Typically, an art project might fit this category. If the project is likely to absorb your child's interest for a long time, have him begin work on it after the more difficult work is completed.

A BETTER PARENTING PRACTICE

A teacher may object to revising homework assignments on the grounds that it is not fair to other students. Remind the teacher that your child has a disability that makes it harder for him to do the same work as the other children. Fair doesn't mean giving every child the same thing, but giving every child what he needs. To be fair, you have to treat a child with learning differences differently.

Difficult work should be attempted only if it is educationally useful to your child. That is, if the assignment seems to be busy work with no apparent purpose, do not force your child to complete it; instead, ask the teacher the purpose of the assignment. Understanding the purpose will provide a guide for development of appropriate modifications. If the assignment seems to be useful for other children, but doesn't help your child—look for an alternative that will achieve the same goal. For example, a teacher may ask that a child write a separate sentence for each word on a spelling list, with the idea that this will help children know the meaning of the words and give them writing practice. For your child, sentence-writing may be so overwhelming that there is no time left to study and learn the spelling words; your child might do better to focus on studying and writing the individual spelling words, and dictating sentences or writing short definitions instead.

You and your child might also find the task of managing homework easier if the teacher will provide a weekly assignment sheet listing all homework to be completed by the end of the week, rather than giving separate assignments each day. This will help you plan for assignments that are likely to be more time consuming by getting an early start and spreading the work out over several days.

Working Effectively with Your Child

Learn to work effectively with your child when helping with homework. Offer help, but don't take over, and by all means do not do the homework for your child. To work effectively, it is important that you are able to communicate well with your child, and that you are able to supply useful strategies to help him overcome barriers.

The first step of good communication is to be able to listen well—do not argue or chastise your child when he says that a task is "too hard" or that he can't understand what the teacher wants. Instead, ask questions to try to find out what is giving him trouble. Keep in mind that children with dyslexia often have difficulty making sense of ordinary language, and your child may need to have an instruction or concept explained or illustrated several different ways before he can understand it.

When helping your child, keep the goals of the homework assignment in mind. If your struggling reader is asked to read and answer questions about a section in his history book, the goal is to learn about history, not reading and writing. In that case, it is fine for you to help by reading the chapter and the questions to your son, and even letting him dictate answers to you if he also has problems with writing.

However, if your child's resource teacher wants him to build fluency by reading a story at home, he needs to do the reading on his own. You can help by sitting next to him as he reads, helping him recognize words that are difficult for him, and listening to him practice reading aloud. When the goal is reading practice, then it is more important that your child work for an appropriate amount of time than to finish the assignment; you can send a note to the teacher letting her know how far your son was able to progress.

It may be useful to have your child work with a sibling or friend for some of her homework. If she is working with another child, observe from a distance to ensure that the children seem to be getting along well. Your child may feel more highly motivated and be more ready to accept constructive criticism from a peer. It is fine for the study partner to offer help and suggestions, but make sure that the other child does not take over and do most of the work or try to correct your child's finished work. In some cases, a younger sibling who is reading at a level close to your child's may be a good study partner.

You may want to hire an older child or teenager to help your child. You shouldn't expect a teenager to have the same skills as an adult teacher or use this as a substitute for getting quality tutoring for your child. Rather, look simply for someone who can establish a good rapport with your child and can work cooperatively with him to help complete assignments.

Using Technology

Computers are your child's best friend. The sooner your child learns to use a word-processing program, the better off he will be. The word-processing program will eliminate a good deal of the frustration that makes writing difficult for individuals with dyslexia. It will eliminate the mechanical barriers your child faces—poor penmanship, bad spelling—enabling him to showcase his ideas through his writing. Although your child may encounter teachers who resist accepting typewritten assignments in elementary years, by the time he reaches high school, his teachers will expect all significant written work to be word typed; often, he is likely to bypass the printer altogether and be asked to submit work via e-mail.

Word-Processing Programs

There are many software programs available to help a young child learn keyboarding skills. While typing is generally a slow process for very young children, it may still be more efficient for your child with dyslexia to use a hunt-and-peck approach than to rely on handwriting, especially if he has difficulty writing legibly. Generally typing speed will improve when the child is about age ten to twelve. Most children want to be able to use computers to access the Internet and play computer games, so your child is likely to be quite willing to work at improving typing skills.

A BETTER PARENTING PRACTICE

Help your child set automatic save options to preserve a copy of his work at frequent intervals. You should also set the program to automatically preserve a backup copy of a document each time it is saved. There is nothing more frustrating to a budding writer than losing the product of several hours' work due to a computer malfunction or keyboarding error.

The company AlphaSmart makes keyboards specifically developed for classroom use that also offers software geared to students with learning disabilities. These allow students to enter and edit text at their school desks. The AlphaSmart Neo costs about $250 and is popular in many schools; it is a good choice for younger children and in classroom settings and a good alternative to more expensive notebook computers.

By the time your child is about age ten, he should be introduced to a regular computer word-processing program. In addition to learning to input text, your child should learn how to use specific features of the program, including the spell checker and grammar checker, and special features like "autocorrect" and automatic text completion options that can simplify text entry and help avoid common spelling and typographical errors.

Using a word-processing program also enables your child to work with his teacher to improve the quality of his writing, through revisions and redrafts. Because the student is spared the laborious process of writing out a second draft by hand, the teacher is free to offer detailed comments and suggestions. Your child will become more confident about writing when he realizes that his first draft does not have to be perfect.

Another advantage of using a computer is that the child can set display options to make it easier to read material—for example, by choosing to view a magnified version of the text—and can also choose a preferred font. Many children with dyslexia are easily confused by different font sets, and so often develop a strong preference for those which seem to be more readable. The Comic Sans font, which comes with Windows systems, is a popular choice partly because of high legibility.

Use of a computer spell checker will also help many children with dyslexia improve their spelling skills. The computer can be set to automatically highlight spelling mistakes, which not only focuses the child's attention on the error, but also requires interactive participation to correct the mistake by choosing the correct alternative from a drop-down list.

Special Software for Dyslexia

You may also be interested in specialized software designed to help individuals with dyslexia. One such program is ReadOn, a software package for Windows, which combines a text-to-speech screen reader with customizable tools to enable reading practice to build visual tracking and reading fluency.

For improved writing, there is a software program called Read & Write made by Texthelp Systems, which is available in both Windows and Mac formats. This is a word-processing program that includes specialized features such as a phonetic spell checker, homophone support, word prediction, dictionary, and pronunciation tutor. The program also includes text-to-speech features which can be set to read aloud words as they are typed in, or to read aloud any text in compatible file formats.

The text-to-speech function is also available through many other inexpensive software formats, including many that are offered for free; some text-to-speech functionality is also built in to Windows Vista and Mac operating systems. A program that also enables speech for website content can be very helpful, especially if your child is a slow reader, when he needs to do Internet research to prepare school papers and projects.

For an older child (about age twelve and older) you may consider getting speech-recognition or dictation software; this will allow your child to use a microphone to dictate into the computer. Two popular packages are Dragon NaturallySpeaking and IBM ViaVoice; Windows Vista also comes with a similar program called Narrator. The drawback with these dictation programs is that the software must be trained to recognize the voice and speech patterns of the user; generally this is done by reading specific passages into the computer. The passages may be difficult for a younger child to read; an older child may also have some difficulty, but is likely to have more patience for the process. Also, although dictating seems like an easy way to get words into print, the user must be able to read well enough to catch and correct some of the more egregious mistakes this software is likely to produce. Although accuracy of the software improves with each new version, it still will transcribe many words erroneously, especially with proper names.

Handheld Devices

Your child may also benefit from handheld dictionaries or spell checkers. A simple and inexpensive product (approximately $20) is the Franklin Spelling Ace, which enables the student to type in a phonetic or guessed spelling in order to find the correct spelling. A child with reading difficulties might prefer a slightly more expensive option with speech capabilities, such as the Children's Talking Dictionary (about $50).

As your child encounters more difficult reading tasks, you might consider the WizCom Reading Pen, which is a handheld device with a small electronic scanner that can scan a word or line of text and read it aloud to the student; it also has a built-in dictionary with definitions of all words. Accuracy is poor for scans of full lines of text, so the tool is not helpful for a child with no reading skills. However, for individual words, accuracy is quite high, and the product's built-in dictionary contains many technical terms that a high school student is likely to encounter in textbook reading. Thus, the Reading Pen can be extremely useful to a student who has difficulty deciphering new and unfamiliar words.

Using Study Guides

As your child grows older, he may also find it helpful to use commercial outlines and study guides. One of the most popular products is SparkNotes, which produces inexpensive study guides in just about every academic subject your child is likely to encounter, and also makes the contents of all its material available free of charge online. The site also has the entire text of many classic literary works available online, as well as supportive study material; with the aid of speech-to-text software this makes a wide array of difficult material very accessible to your struggling reader. Some materials are also now available in audio format.

Be alert to improper use of such materials, however. One drawback of modern technology and the wide array of support materials available to your child is that it makes cheating very easy. As your child's sophistication with computers grows, he will soon discover the ease with which he can cut and paste text from Internet resources and reference software.

Your child should not be deprived of access to resources and technology that will enable him to learn merely because of the risk that he may misuse them. Rather, it is important that you discuss with him your own expectations about intellectual honesty, as well as legal and ethical concerns. Many children simply do not know or understand that it is wrong to copy or paraphrase material from websites; others simply are overwhelmed with their workload and feel they have no choice but to take short cuts. A child with a learning disability is far more likely to be tempted to copy others' work.

You can help by continuing to supervise your child's work and being an active participant in the writing process. Offer to proofread your child's written work, both as a way of helping your child, and so that you are aware of what his original work looks like and have an opportunity to see work that he is turning in.

A BETTER PARENTING PRACTICE

If it appears that your child has copied passages of his work from the Internet, take the time to discuss with him the importance of putting information into his own words. Most children with dyslexia are highly creative thinkers; compliment your child whenever possible on his originality of thought and encourage him to voice his own opinions in his writing.

Keep in mind that until your child overcomes all aspects of his reading disability, he is at a disadvantage in comparison to his peers for reading and writing assignments. Your child is as intelligent as his classmates and should be entitled to the same quality of education. For him, books on tape, videos, and study guides are necessary tools that will afford him access to the same quality of learning as children who are stronger readers. If your eighth grader receives tutoring because he reads at a third grade level, he cannot reasonably be expected to read *Huckleberry Finn* on his own. His mind is ready to appreciate the rich vocabulary and complex themes presented in the book, and he will certainly learn far more by listening to an audio book and watching a movie than by trying to struggle through text he can barely decipher. This alternative is far preferable to reading an abridged, limited-vocabulary version of the book, or being denied the educational benefit of advanced literature while consigned to reading material geared to third graders. No teacher would deny a blind student the opportunity to rely on recorded books; if your child does not have the ability to read at a level equivalent to his intellectual ability to understand, he should be entitled to use whatever forms of educational aids are available.

As a parent, it is important for you to help your child learn to strike an appropriate balance between reading on his own and using technology and available media to supplement his learning. Make clear to your child that you expect him to be honest about letting you and his teachers know when he has relied on supportive material. Keep in mind that reliance on such support will help your child develop a more advanced vocabulary and thinking skills that will, in turn, allow him to develop into a better reader. Scientific research shows that individuals with dyslexia rely heavily on the thinking and problem-solving frontal areas of their brains for reading; these areas will be developed as your child is exposed to advanced literature and concepts through other means.

Chapter 9

Avoiding Academic Barriers

Ten Things You Will Learn in This Chapter

- Why rote memorization is difficult for your child.

- Why your child may have trouble learning math facts.

- How routine classroom practices may work to punish your child for having dyslexia.

- Modifications that will help your child learn more efficiently.

- Ways to help your child keep track of his school assignments.

- How to work with your child's teacher to ensure fair grading practices.

- Why standardized testing is not a good way to measure your child's progress.

- Why grade retention usually harms children.

- What circumstances might warrant retention.

- Alternatives to grade retention that will help your child learn.

Speed Contests and Rote Learning

Even though your child is legally entitled to be free from discrimination and may also qualify for special education services, he is still likely to encounter many academic barriers at school. Some will be major barriers, such as requirements that he perform successfully on standardized tests. Others will be less significant, focused on single or short-term classroom assignments, but may nonetheless cause considerable frustration.

Unfortunately, a good deal of teaching in elementary school and middle school involves rote memorization, often with an emphasis on speed. Your child's dyslexia is not merely a reading issue; it also is reflected in the speed with which he processes linguistic information or translates his thoughts into written or oral expression. Even when your child knows an answer, he is likely to freeze up, become forgetful, or make many mistakes when under pressure to answer quickly.

Typically, your child will be expected to memorize math facts and multiplication tables, usually quizzed in a format emphasizing speed, such as the "mad minute" where children are assessed based on how quickly they can solve simple math problems. Your child will probably be given weekly lists of ten to twenty spelling words to master; as he grows older these will be replaced by vocabulary lists, with word definitions to memorize. Your child will also be expected to memorize facts such as historical dates or state capitals, or lines of poetry or famous speeches.

A BETTER PARENTING PRACTICE

Work with your child's teacher to help her understand that assignments that call for rote memorization of isolated facts are particularly difficult for your child. Your child will learn much better if she can study subjects in depth, and can relate facts to other knowledge that explains their significance. Encourage the teacher to provide alternative assignments related to the subject area that will give your child an opportunity to shine.

All of these tasks rely on strong verbal and linguistic skills. Even the rote memorization of math facts is a linguistic, not a mathematical, skill. None of these tasks is particularly important to your child's ultimate educational success: not only can your child figure out or look up this information if memory fails him, but the need to memorize many of these facts has been rendered obsolete by modern technology. This doesn't mean that these skills shouldn't be taught to those children who can easily master them—but it does mean that you can and should arrange modifications such as alternative assignments or extended time for your child as needed.

School Privileges and Punishments

Even if your child has an IEP or a written 504 plan, you may find that he is denied privileges or punished in subtle ways at school because of his learning problems. For example, a teacher may allow all children who have finished their classwork free time to play games every Friday afternoon; the other children may be sent to the library or a study hall to finish their assignments. Of course, your child never gets any free play time, as his slower reading speed and labored writing makes it impossible for him to complete assignments early. Similar difficulties may also lead to specific punishments, such as being held inside for recess, denied permission to attend a school assembly, or held after school. You may even find that your child is being punished, or denied privileges, by being forced to make up assignments that he missed because he was pulled out of class to work with the resource teacher.

DOES THIS SOUND LIKE YOUR CHILD?

Your child may not tell you about the day-to-day slights and inconveniences he suffers because of his dyslexia. He may not understand himself that many of his difficulties are directly related to his learning differences, and he may feel embarrassed about the treatment he endures at school, or fear your disapproval if he confesses additional failings. Although frustrated, he may perceive the teacher's rules as "fair" because they are equally applied to other students, and may be reluctant to ask for special treatment.

In some cases, your child may suffer negative consequences because of problems that are not directly related to her reading ability. Many children with dyslexia have poor organizational skills; your daughter may habitually misplace her homework or forget to write down assignments. Her language processing issues may lead her to frequently misunderstand instructions, or miss "hearing" them altogether. Your child's teacher may not understand how the reading problem relates to problems with focusing attention, listening, following instructions, or keeping track of deadlines and paperwork.

You may need to work to educate the teacher about your child's limitations, and arrange for appropriate modifications in your child's IEP or 504 plan. You might point out to the teacher that her "rules" end up singling out the same students week after week for punishment or denial of privileges, and thus are not effective as incentives to change behavior. Ask for informal modifications that will give your child a chance to rectify the problems, such as reduced volume of work, or the opportunity to work on finishing assignments over the weekend.

Helping with Organizational Skills

You can also work at home to help your child develop stronger organizational skills—an area often missed at school. Provide your child with a planner that he can use to track assignments; ask the teacher to check his planner each day or week to make sure that he has everything correctly noted. If the teacher is unwilling to aid your child this way, help your child find a classroom buddy who can help track the homework—pick a child who is reliable, has good attendance and grades, and encourage your child to regularly check with his buddy to make sure he is on track. If your child is embarrassed to ask or has a hard time making friends, consider hiring another child to be your child's "secretary"—for a few dollars a week you may gain a trusted ally for your own child.

A BETTER PARENTING PRACTICE

Use incentives at home to help keep your child on track, providing positive reinforcement rather than punishment or loss of privileges. Set more reasonable and smaller, short-term goals for your child, and offer small rewards such as extra play time when those goals are reached. Organizational skills are partly a matter of habit, and habits must be practiced repeatedly over time before they become ingrained.

Help your child keep organized at home, as well. Use a large wall calendar in a prominent place in your home, such as the kitchen or dining area, to track appointments and events, including homework deadlines and reminders. Create a filing system using colored folders or binders to keep track of your child's work; keep this near his regular study area, and help him learn to keep his papers filed in the appropriate "to do" or subject folder, rather than left loose in his backpack or bedroom.

Also encourage your child to keep graded papers that have been returned to him in a file folder or binder for each subject, so he can review the papers later when preparing for exams. This will also prove useful if the teacher mistakenly fails to record a grade for completed work. Your child's ability to easily produce the completed assignment from home may avoid having to repeat work unnecessarily.

Assessment and Grading

Your child may be able to learn most of the material covered in class, but may still face barriers when it comes to the way that his work is assessed and grades are assigned. Traditionally, grades are assigned based on uniform criteria for all children in a class, often reflecting how a child measures up to his peers. It is a competitive process that may give little information about what the individual child has actually learned. It sets up children with learning difficulties for repeated failure, because no matter how hard they work, they are unlikely to be able to earn high marks. This system not only undermines your child's self-esteem, but also contributes to behavior problems.

Along with modifications to curriculum, you can suggest and encourage the teacher to use alternative forms of assessment. The best approaches will factor in your child's demonstrated effort and her level of improvement over time. The teacher can use records of past performance, such as with spelling or arithmetic, as a way of determining the level of performance that can reasonably be expected of your child. Improved performance should result in an improved grade—for example, if a child who usually gets seven correct answers out of twenty problems is able to increase performance to ten, the child's improvement should be recognized and rewarded.

Ask the teacher to mark your child's paper in a positive way, noting correct answers prominently. The teacher can score the papers by simply counting the number or percentage of right answers on homework assignments or quizzes, recording those in her grade book. If a pattern of improvement is seen, the teacher can help your child chart his progress; at the end of the term, a grade can be assigned that is consistent with the level of improvement.

The teacher can also modify grading practices to specifically exempt certain considerations for your child. For example, the teacher can agree to disregard spelling mistakes in all subjects other than spelling. Thus your child would be graded on the content of his written essays or answers to questions, not on the mechanics of producing them.

Once the teacher has agreed on modifications for your child, it is helpful if the teacher can create a specific rubric for grading his work. A rubric is a set of written requirements listing the specific criteria to earn a passing grade of A, B, C, and so forth. If the teacher generally uses a rubric for the whole class, modifications can simply be noted on your child's copy.

In addition to ensuring that agreed-upon modifications will be considered in assigning a grade, a well-drafted rubric will also help improve your child's performance. For example, a rubric that indicates that writing two paragraphs can only earn a "C," but writing three or more paragraphs will earn a "B," might provide your child with the incentive to work hard to complete an extra paragraph, as he can clearly connect his extra effort to the reward of a higher grade. It also gives your child a greater sense of control, and enables him to better understand how the grade relates to the quality of his work.

High-Stakes Testing

High-stakes testing is the practice of using a single, standardized test to make important decisions about a student's education, usually whether the child will be promoted to the next grade, or be allowed to graduate from high school. Such tests tend to work in a discriminatory fashion against students with dyslexia, both because of the content of the test and the method of assessment. At least through eighth grade level, these tests almost always are focused largely on appraising reading and math skills; by definition, a child with dyslexia can be expected to have weaker reading skills. But even after gaining skills, the timed, multiple-choice format works against students who have a history of dyslexia; many such students become capable readers and strong students, but continue to perform poorly on standardized tests. Thus, the high-stakes test is a double barrier for your child.

Misuse of Standardized Tests

Many states and individual school districts impose strict testing and grade retention policies because of political or social pressure to increase standards among their students. The practice of social promotion—promoting children to maintain age/grade level regardless of level of achievement—can lead to children being passed from one level to the next in school without learning anything. Obviously, this is not an acceptable outcome for any child. However, retention policies do nothing to improve the quality of teaching.

Unfortunately, schools often misuse standardized tests to make grade retention decisions, applying their results for purposes where they are not valid. The most common problem is using norm-referenced group tests to measure individual achievement. These tests are designed to provide a good statistical sampling of how a particular school's students score when measured against typical students. However, the norm-referenced tests developed for assessing school performance are not valid as a measure of individual progress and performance. In some cases, they may contain questions about material that has not been covered in your child's school. While it is valid to criticize the school for failing to teach content appropriate for each grade level, it is not appropriate to draw conclusions about your child's abilities based on subject areas where he may not have received adequate instruction.

DID YOU KNOW?

A *norm-referenced* test compares a student's score against the scores of a group of students who have already taken the same exam, called the "norming group." Some widely used tests are the California Achievement Test (CAT), Comprehensive Test of Basic Skills (CTBS), Iowa Test of Basic Skills (ITBS) and Tests of Academic Proficiency (TAP), Metropolitan Achievement Test (MAT), and Stanford Achievement Test (SAT).

Even on subject matter that has been covered in class, the group norm-referenced test is ordinarily not designed to measure individual ability or achievement. In many cases, missing a single question can cause a big change in an individual student's percentile rank. The designers of these tests try to choose questions that are useful to sort students along a curve. Many items that most students in a grade level would be expected to know are not tested, and questions may be deliberately designed to focus on more obscure knowledge, in order to help rank the students. Thus, there is too much left to chance—and too much material that is not included in the test—for the test to give a good picture of your child's abilities.

When the test results of many students are considered cumulatively, as is done to measure school performance, individual variation loses significance, and the tests can give a good general picture of how well the students at the particular school perform in comparison to nationally expected averages. But when the same test is used to measure your child, the test is simply being misused.

Further, on a test of reading achievement, it is unfair and unreasonable to expect your child with dyslexia to score well against a norm-referenced standard. By definition, children with dyslexia will usually score significantly below average for reading skills—in fact, it is likely that your child only qualifies for services at your school by virtue of such low skills. The concept of "grade level reading" is by itself an expression of a norm, or average; it reflects what the typical, or mid-range, student is expected to be able to achieve at each grade. It is neither reasonable nor possible to expect that every child will perform at or above average; statistical analysis will always place students along a curve with the weakest of the group falling along the tail end.

It is a reasonable goal to expect a child with dyslexia to eventually achieve reading proficiency; many will in fact become good readers. It is not reasonable to expect your child to read the same as a "normal" child at the same age or to somehow radically increase his performance when measured against other students within a single year. Thus, your child's reading achievement should be measured using criterion-based tests—that is, tests that measure many skill areas without reference to how your child's performance compares with others.

College Entrance Exams

If your child is considering college, he will usually need to take college entrance exams. Most colleges will accept either the ACT Assessment or the College Board SAT. Some colleges also require that students take several subject-specific exams, called the SAT II.

The ACT Assessment covers topics in English, math, reading, and science reasoning; there is also an optional written essay that is required by many colleges. The ACT is scored by counting all right answers, without deducting points for wrong answers; thus there is no penalty for guessing. Also, ACT reports only test results from a specific test administration; the student designates which test score will be sent to the college. Thus, a student can take the test on several occasions and choose to only report her highest score.

The SAT includes three separate sections on Writing, Critical Reading, and Math. The Writing section includes multiple-choice questions on grammar and usage, and a student-written essay. Under a new policy, which will be implemented in 2009, students have the option of choosing whether to submit all of the test scores from multiple sittings, or to choose which scores to submit to colleges.

Your child may be eligible for accommodations while taking these exams, such as extra time to complete the exam, large print test booklets, or use of audiocassettes with the exam questions. However, you should check well in advance as to the current requirements for obtaining such modifications. Generally, a written request must be submitted before the registration deadline, and must be supported by a professional diagnosis of a learning disability and evidence that your child has received similar modifications at school through an IEP or 504 plan.

Avoiding Grade Retention

If your child struggles in school, it is likely that at some point a teacher or school official will recommend that he be retained and repeat a grade. Grade retention is almost never a good idea for a child with dyslexia, as the possible negative consequences far outweigh the benefits. Dyslexia is not something that can be out-grown or cured by waiting for a child to mature; repeating the same curriculum a second time around will not help your child improve his basic skills.

What the Research Shows

Retention is far more likely to hurt your child than help him; this is especially true in the early elementary years. Dozens of research studies conducted over many years show that students who are retained because they are performing poorly usually fall even further behind over time. Children who are promoted despite concerns about their academic skills may still have difficulties, but their performance is usually somewhat better than their counterparts who have been retained.

Of course, statistics don't tell the whole story—some children do benefit from retention. However, research-ers have found that the students who benefit usually have mastered reading skills, and had been held back for other reasons, such as a large amount of absenteeism or a midyear transfer to a new school. In other words, a student who is a capable learner but needs to make up for missed instruction may benefit from repeating a grade; a student with learning difficulties needs a differ-ent sort of help.

The long-term effects of grade retention can be dev-astating. Students who are retained for a year are more likely to later drop out of school, even when compared to students with equally poor performance. Retention can also be emotionally traumatizing. In one study, 84 percent of retained first graders said they felt "bad" or "sad" or "upset" about the retention and many reported being teased by their peers. In another recent study, children indicated that they believed grade retention was the worst thing that could happen to them, even worse than losing a parent or going blind.

DID YOU KNOW?

Studies show that grade retention increases the likelihood that your child will not complete high school by as much as 40 percent; if your child is retained more than once, there is an almost 100 percent likelihood that he will later drop out.

Studies of middle and high school students also demonstrate a high social cost of retention; students who are old for their grade level reported higher levels of emotional distress, substance abuse, involvement with violence, and suicidal thoughts. No matter how well-intentioned, holding a child back a year can send the message that he is a failure, and that the teachers do not believe him capable of keeping up with his peers.

When Retention Is Appropriate

The only time you should favor retention is if you have positive answers in your own mind to the questions "What will be different in the coming year?" and "What plan is in place that will help my child learn in the coming year?" If retention will make your child eligible for services that she cannot receive with promotion—for example, if promotion means moving on to a different school site, or if there is a specialized program only available to children in certain grade levels—the prospect may be more appealing.

You may favor retention if your child will be placed with a specific teacher that you feel is particularly well-qualified to help your child, either because of the teacher's reputation or because of specialized training she may have. Consider your child's feelings as well—in some cases, a child may prefer retention because of fears or uncertainty about her ability to perform in the next grade. While such fears should not be the sole consideration, often children have valid reasons for their concerns that should be explored.

You may also consider retention if your child is moving to a new school where the curriculum or standards are somewhat different—in that case, while the child may stay at the same grade level, he is not truly "repeating" a grade. This situation is common when children move from public to private schools, as many private schools have a more demanding curriculum. Some parents have also found it valuable to delay entrance into middle school or high school for a year, homeschooling their child in the interim. Because of social ramifications, this choice should only be made when the child agrees to the plan.

Alternatives to Retention

The best alternative to retention is appropriate, specialized help for your child's learning difficulties, combined with appropriate modifications and support to enable your child to keep up in academic subjects other than reading. If your child already has an IEP, it may be appropriate to review the IEP and reconsider the goals set and the specific educational services being provided, rather than hold your child back.

Kindergarten and Entering First Grade

If retention is suggested because of your child's poor reading skills or apparent lack of reading readiness, you should immediately ask that your child be assessed if she has not already been diagnosed with a learning disability. Do not accept the teacher's opinion that your child is merely immature or needs an extra year—even if the teacher turns out to be right, the apparent need for retention is a red flag that your child should be evaluated. Follow the procedures outlined in Chapter 3 to request and obtain special education services through the school.

If your child is still in kindergarten, consider both his actual age and social fit. Although the practice of holding children back to repeat a year of kindergarten is very common in many districts, there is no research evidence proving that this will help. However, many of the studies reporting long-term deleterious effects of retention focus on the child being old for his grade. If your child is one of the younger children in his class, there may be no harm in repeating kindergarten, particularly if he seems socially immature or unready for the behavioral expectations of first grade.

However, it is still important that your child be evaluated for learning disabilities. Keep in mind that some early intervention strategies—particularly phonemic awareness training—seem to lose effectiveness if delayed past the age of seven. Find out what services your school offers to first grade students, and ask whether your child can receive the services with a repeated year that he might also get if promoted.

Beyond First Grade

At first grade level and above, you should not agree to retention based on concerns about your child's academic skill level if your child will simply be repeating the same curriculum in the same basic setting. Your child does not need more of the same instruction; he needs a different approach. Tutoring and remedial teaching can be provided to a promoted child as easily as it can be to a retained child, and your child is likely to be more motivated and engaged in school if being introduced to new material.

DID YOU KNOW?

The National Association of School Psychologists strongly cautions against grade retention, and recommends that struggling students be promoted along with a plan of special interventions, accommodations, and services geared to the specific academic areas where they are struggling.

One alternative to retention is to place your child in a transitional classroom with an enriched curriculum designed to lead to double promotion, with the intent that after the transitional year she will catch up with her age cohorts. It is possible that even without such a classroom, an IEP could be written to effectively serve the same goals.

In some schools, you may be able to arrange partial acceleration or retention—that is, a combined approach where your child moves on to the next grade for some or all subjects, but leaves the classroom to work with the lower grade for areas where there are specific skill deficits, usually reading or arithmetic. This should not be used in lieu of specialized remedial help, but is something to consider if it is clear that your child will not be able to keep up even with accommodations in isolated subject areas.

Some elementary schools have mixed-age, ungraded or combined grade classrooms. Often such schools have overlapping grades—for example, one classroom may have a grade three/four combination, with a four/five grade combination in another classroom. In such a setting, the decision to keep your child with the "lower" grade combination is not the same as retention—teachers in such an environment are used to having students for more than one year and teaching a varied curriculum. If your child has been doing well with a particular teacher, he may benefit from staying with that teacher another year. Conversely, if he has not been doing well, it may be time for a change, even if it seems illogical to push the child into the more difficult level.

Chapter 10

School Choices from Kindergarten Through College

Ten Things You Will Learn in This Chapter

- Factors to consider in choosing a school.
- Advantages of Montessori or Waldorf schools.
- What to look for in a private school.
- Information about specialized schools for dyslexia.
- When homeschooling may be a good choice.
- Choices to be made at the high school level.
- Ways to promote success when studying a foreign language.
- Planning for college and beyond.
- Alternatives to regular high schools.
- How to guide your child toward success in choosing a career.

Choosing a School for Your Child

Although many children with dyslexia can do well in a traditional school environment with appropriate support and accommodations, you may decide to explore different options for your child. If your child is struggling, you may want to find a school that offers special support for dyslexia, or a more nurturing environment that better fits his personality and educational needs.

Charter and Magnet Schools

Many public school districts offer excellent choices in addition to the regular schools. These may be labeled as charter, alternative, or magnet schools. In general such schools receive public funding and must meet some guidelines of your district, but are free to use a different curriculum and teaching strategies. Magnet schools usually offer a special focus such as arts or science and technology. The philosophies and programs of these schools cover a wide spectrum, ranging from schools that are highly structured and offer a challenging academic curriculum, to schools that are innovative and focus on creating a hands-on, child-centered environment.

Consider your child's interests and strengths when you choose a school. Of course you will want to consider what services each school offers for children with dyslexia, and whether the curriculum used will fit your child's needs. But it is a mistake to focus exclusively on your child's areas of weaknesses, because ideally you want a school where your child will be happy, will be able to make friends, and will enjoy participating in school activities beyond the classroom.

Private Schools

You may feel that a private school can better meet your child's unique learning needs. Many private schools are very sensitive to the needs of children with learning differences. Some things to look for in a private school are:

- **Small classes.** Your child may do better in a school that offers smaller classes and a higher teacher-to-student ratio than most public schools.
- **Flexible educational approach.** Your child can do well in almost any environment, if the adults who work with her are willing to adjust their expectations and modify teaching when appropriate.
- **Enrichment and special interest programs.** A private school may offer enrichment or special instruction in areas of high interest to your child, such as the arts or music, athletic programs, or enrichment activities geared to gifted students.

However, you should keep in mind that unlike public schools, private schools are under no legal obligation to provide special educational services for your child. Teachers at a private school with a strong academic program may be unwilling to make special accommodations for your struggling child. Although you may still be eligible for services via the public school district, you may find it impracticable to arrange for your child to receive those services while attending the private school.

A BETTER PARENTING PRACTICE

You naturally want the best for your child. However, even if it is clear that your child is exceptionally bright, you should avoid placing him in a highly structured or academically demanding private school unless it is clear that the school will be sensitive to his learning needs, and provide extra support where needed. Your child will do better in the long run if he learns in a nurturing environment where he can experience success.

Some social and emotional issues that accompany dyslexia may manifest as classroom behavioral issues. Your child might be a physically active, kinesthetic learner, always on the move—but to a teacher, he may seem like a troublemaker who refuses to stay in his seat. A private school is not legally obligated to retain a student whose behavior is disruptive, or who is unable to keep up academically. Whereas in public school you could arrange via an IEP for specific classroom modifications to address your child's unique learning needs, in a private setting your child may simply be subjected to repeated discipline and eventually asked to leave the school.

Montessori Schools

Montessori is a child-centered, hands-on, individualized approach to learning based on the philosophy of Maria Montessori, an Italian physician and educator. In the early part of the twentieth century, Dr. Montessori developed an array of self-teaching physical materials, such as puzzles or stacking blocks, to assist children who had been labeled as mentally defective. Within two years, the children learned to read and were able to pass the standard tests given at public schools for their age level. Dr. Montessori had invented the first "multisensory" approach to teaching; the handicapped children that she worked with would likely be diagnosed with dyslexia, high-functioning autism, or related learning disabilities by today's standards. The materials worked equally well for very young children, and over the years Montessori became widely known as an academic approach well-suited for the developmental needs of preschool-age children.

Montessori schools allow children to discover concepts through self-guided work under the supervision of specially trained teachers. Children are introduced to the letters of the alphabet by learning the sounds of each letter, and running their fingers over sandpaper cutouts of the letters. They prepare for writing by tracing insets or stencils of simple shapes, like circles and triangles, until they have the manual dexterity to manage letters as well. Most will learn to write before they can read, encouraged by the teacher to piece together letter blocks or cutouts on their own to form words. This phonetic approach begins at age two; a child is never pushed or prodded by the teacher, but simply allowed to progress at his own individual pace.

Children in a Montessori environment are kept in mixed-age groups, such as ages two to five, or six to nine. At the elementary and middle school level, Montessori continues to be highly individualized, allowing each child to work at his own level, but there is more focus on group work as older children are better able to work and learn cooperatively with their peers.

Waldorf Schools

Waldorf Schools follow the philosophy of Rudolf Steiner, who felt that schools should encourage children's natural creativity and free-thinking. There is a strong emphasis on arts and music, with formal reading instruction delayed until second or third grade level. During the early years, emphasis is placed on developing oral language skills through storytelling, and academic subjects are introduced via artistic media. Children typically learn to play a musical instrument, spend time gardening, and are exposed to foreign languages. Textbooks are avoided, but children maintain their own workbooks and diaries for each subject. No grades are given at the elementary level; instead the teacher writes a detailed evaluation of each child at the end of each school year.

A Waldorf school can provide a safe and nurturing environment. The emphasis on art projects and imaginative play provides a realm where your child can flourish emotionally and learn through the sensory pathways that best fit his learning style. On the other hand, few

Waldorf teachers will be prepared to help your child if he does not naturally transition into reading at age nine or ten. It may also be harder to determine whether your child will need extra support in an environment where reading instruction is delayed for all children.

Specialized Schools for Dyslexia

There are many excellent private schools geared to students with dyslexia. Most of these schools offer remedial teaching based on traditional Orton-Gillingham principles, as well as providing a full academic curriculum. Some schools are geared primarily to helping their students gain sufficient proficiency in reading and other academic skills to reenter mainstream schools. Others are intended to provide a comprehensive and high-quality education with the expectation that they will retain students through completion of their educational program. Some innovative programs are geared to both dyslexia and gifted education, combining remediation with enrichment and acceleration. Others offer strong programs in arts and hands-on activities geared to the creative strengths of their students.

Homeschooling

Many parents feel they can best meet the needs of their children through homeschooling. If you choose to homeschool, you will be able to provide your child with the individualized attention that is important for a child with dyslexia, and create an educational plan that fits his needs exactly. You will be able to give your child the extra time he needs to master subjects and skills that are difficult for him, and allow him to forge ahead in his areas of strength. Your child will not face the humiliation or daily frustration of classroom failure.

DID YOU KNOW?

In 2003, an estimated 1.1 million students nationwide, or about 3 percent of all students, were being homeschooled. Homeschooling families have a far greater percentage of both gifted as well as learning-disabled students than the national average.

However, homeschooling takes work, and it isn't the ideal situation for every family. You will need to consider carefully whether you can successfully take on the dual role of parent and teacher, knowing that your child may present some unique challenges. Your child's style of learning and communication may be very different from yours, and you may find yourself frustrated when your child does not learn at the pace you would expect.

To succeed with homeschooling, you will need to live by three rules: patience, flexibility, and fun. Patience means the willingness to give your child the time she needs to explore and master a subject, even if that means that a lesson you think should take twenty minutes ends up spread over many days or weeks. Flexibility means the willingness to learn new things and change approaches. You must be ready to change course if your child has difficulty, to listen to and observe your child, to allow her interests and inclinations to guide you, and to learn by trial and error which learning strategies seem most effective. Fun means that you need to always keep your sense of humor, and mix the work of learning with play. Be creative: Use games, puzzles, songs, rhymes, or physical activity. Your child will learn best when she is engaged and eager to participate.

Your Teenager—the High School Years

High school is a time for tremendous physical, intellectual, and emotional growth and exploration. Your teenager will find his school life now includes an expanded array of social, athletic, and extracurricular activities, as well as an enticing choice of elective courses. He experiences a changing relationship with teachers, and is likely to find some who are able to challenge and motivate him, as well as to experience problems with others. The choices he makes now have direct and lasting impact on his adult life. He may find that with his greater maturity and ability to shape his own education, his academic life becomes easier. On the other hand, you may be the parent of a teen who was previously able to cope well despite his dyslexia, but now suddenly finds himself overwhelmed by increased demands for reading and writing and meeting multiple deadlines for his different classes.

Choosing a High School

If you live in a larger community or urban area, your teen may have the choice of several different high school programs. The choice of high school can be an important turning point in your teen's life, because he may be able to choose a school that more closely meets his individual needs or focuses on a program geared to his interests.

Many communities have magnet schools or specialized schools, such as schools with a focus on the visual or performing arts, an emphasis on science and technology, or a strong college preparatory curriculum. Because of the high correlation of dyslexia with creativity, schools with a focus on arts often have a large population of kids with learning styles similar to your teen's, even if they are not formally diagnosed with dyslexia. Attending a school where the students share a common interest may help keep your teen motivated, and foster stronger friendships with his peers.

DOES THIS SOUND LIKE YOUR CHILD?

Even though your child may have had academic difficulties in the past, do not allow a school counselor to dissuade your child from following a college preparatory track if she thinks she may want to attend college. Your child's motivation is the key to her success; she should use her high school education to lay the groundwork for her future educational or career objectives.

Alternatives to Regular High School

If your teen continues to struggle with academics or seems to lack motivation to complete a college preparatory curriculum, he may want to choose a vocational high school. These high schools will provide training geared to giving your child marketable skills, as well as including a basic academic curriculum. Many skills can be taught at the high school level; some examples include electronics, graphic design, television production, carpentry, cosmetology, culinary arts, horticulture, information technology, automotive, child care, architectural drafting, data processing, telecommunications, and marketing. Usually the classes given in the student's chosen area of concentration are hands-on and very practically oriented. Attending a vocational high school can be a rewarding experience for a student who is uncertain about her academic interests and abilities, and provide a needed boost to self-confidence as well as an entry to employment.

Many school districts also have alternative or continuation high schools. These are schools that usually serve students who have become disenchanted with the regular high school environment. These schools focus on building student self-esteem and helping to get disaffected high schoolers back on track. Generally faculty-student ratio is quite low and the schools are very small compared to regular high schools. The goal of these schools is to provide students who are not able to function well in the traditional high school environment with the counseling and teaching needed to earn a high school diploma. If your teenager is in danger of failing or considering dropping out of high school, the alternative high school environment may be the place where he is able to regroup and salvage his education.

Studying a Foreign Language

Many high schools require students to study at least two years of a foreign language, and colleges may prefer students who have three or four years of language study. Students with dyslexia often encounter difficulties when studying a new language. For this reason, many students seek an exemption from foreign language requirements.

However there are many ways that your child can benefit from study of a foreign language. Many students will find that their reading and spelling in English improves after studying a language such as French or Spanish, as they become more aware of the Latin-based roots and structure of English words. Students with dyslexia also sometimes find it easier to read material in a foreign language that is phonetically consistent, such as Spanish.

Choosing a Language

If your child has a choice of languages, try to learn about each of the teachers at the school and the methods they use. Your child may do better in a class where the emphasis is on learning oral conversational skills, and students are taught in an interactive setting, with games and songs used to keep kids motivated. On the other hand, your child may encounter significant barriers if the teacher expects the students to memorize a lot of material and learn primarily through reading, or places great emphasis on writing and learning correct grammar.

DID YOU KNOW?

The most popular languages taught in U.S. high schools or colleges are Spanish, French, German, Italian, Japanese, Latin, Russian, Hebrew, and American Sign Language. Of the above, only French and German have phonetically irregular spellings.

Some factors to consider with each language are:

- Your child's level of motivation to learn the particular language.
- Whether your child already has some familiarity with or exposure to the language.
- Whether the language uses the Roman alphabet or a different alphabet.
- Whether the language is written in a phonetically consistent manner.
- The relative ease or difficulty of pronunciation of words in each language.
- The relative complexity of the grammatical system.
- Your child's preferred mode of learning and his individual pattern of strengths and weaknesses.

Some students who anticipate difficulty with learning to speak a language prefer Latin. Most studies of Latin will involve written texts, and learning Latin generally helps in understanding roots of many English words, which in turn may increase reading comprehension and fluency. American Sign Language is another very popular alternative for students with dyslexia, who generally find it easy and fun to learn a language made up of gestures rather than words.

Participatory Language Approaches

Despite concerns that foreign language instruction will be a barrier for learners with dyslexia, many students have successfully gained fluency in multiple languages. Individuals with dyslexia are usually able to acquire basic conversational abilities in a new language within a reasonable time after moving to countries where the language is spoken. The problems typically experienced with classroom learning may simply reflect the failure of traditional teaching methods, which often rely heavily on rote memorization or listening and repetition of short phrases.

Total Physical Response Method

Total Physical Response (TPR) is a method for foreign language learning that attempts to replicate the natural way that small children learn to speak and understand language. It incorporates physical movement and gestures in an immersion environment; the teacher speaks only the language being taught, while using gestures to help convey meaning. In the beginning, the teacher gives simple commands that require some sort of movement from the students. Later, the class incorporates more complex interactive activities, such as acting out skits and playing games, but always there is some sort of movement or response from the student.

With TPR, students are not required to speak the language until they do so spontaneously; usually this happens after several weeks or a few months in the classroom. Written forms of the language are not introduced until students have developed a good oral understanding. This method was originally developed by James Asher, a university professor interested in studying brain-based processes of learning. Dr. Asher believes that all learning is enhanced by methods that integrate left and right brain hemispheric processing, an idea similar to Dr. Samuel Orton's reasoning in developing multisensory methods for dyslexia. The TPR method is widely known among foreign language teachers; many incorporate some TPR ideas even if they do not rely solely on the method.

Language Learning Software

Your child may find it helpful to use Rosetta Stone software system, which is used in many schools and colleges and is also available for home use. This system is available for about thirty different languages, and is highly interactive; the student listens to a set of foreign words and phrases while looking at pictures depicting their meaning. Then, when the student feels ready, there is a computer quiz, during which the student must choose the picture that matches the word from a set of four illustrations. As the student's proficiency increases, the level of difficulty rises. The student can opt to look at written words as well as to listen to the language, and the software also affords speaking practice using a microphone and voice recognition software. The computer gamelike setting allows the student to control the pace; in most cases the student rapidly gains a strong vocabulary.

Choosing a College

Many students with dyslexia go on to college, even if they have struggled with academics during their elementary and high school years. Even the most prestigious and highly selective colleges will provide accommodations for students with learning disabilities, so dyslexia should not be a barrier. However, it is important for your teenager to consider his own learning style and preferences. He may find that he prefers a college with flexible graduation requirements, or he may want a college where class sizes are small to allow close interaction between students and instructors.

There are literally hundreds of excellent colleges your child can choose from. Many have very lenient admission standards, and will accept your child even if he has received mostly Bs and Cs in high school. Attending a smaller, less well-known college can be a distinct advantage for a student who sometimes struggles with learning, as the school environment may be less competitive and the instructors more willing to provide support and guidance.

A growing number of colleges do not require students to submit standardized test scores. Colleges are becoming increasingly aware that such test scores are of dubious value in predicting success rates, especially because they often reflect the level of student preparation through coaching or studying for the test, rather than school achievement. Many students with dyslexia simply do not ever test well, whether or not they receive accommodations.

DID YOU KNOW?

The National Center for Fair and Open Testing has compiled a list of more than 750 four-year colleges and universities nationwide that admit a substantial number of students without regard to test scores. Their list, available at *www.fairtest.org*, includes a wide variety of institutions, from small, private liberal arts colleges to large, public universities.

Because of provisions of the Americans with Disabilities Act and Section 504, almost every college will make some provisions for students with learning disabilities; the only colleges exempt from the federal legal requirements are some small religious colleges that do not accept any federal funding or benefits for their students. However, the law requires only that colleges make "reasonable accommodations" for students; it neither dictates what is "reasonable" nor mandates extra support services. The level and type of support can be very different from one institution to the next. Thus, it is important to ask about special programs and support services available at each college your teen is considering. Be sure to ask about the types of assistance your child is most likely to need, such as arrangements for students who need help taking notes or writing papers, or availability of recorded books.

Career Planning

A young person with dyslexia can be successful with just about any career he chooses. In many cases, compensation strategies used to cope with continuing reading difficulties turn out to be an asset. David Boies, a trial lawyer known for his exceptional courtroom skills, attributes his prodigious memory in part to reading difficulties—he learned to rely on memory in order to avoid the need to read transcripts of testimony or re-read law books. Many actors with dyslexia report similar experiences with memorizing their lines: they simply don't want to have to read the script a second time, so they get it right on the first try.

DID YOU KNOW?

A survey of 300 self-made millionaires found that 40 percent had been diagnosed with dyslexia. A larger survey of 5,000 millionaires found that more than half reported early struggles in school. Some highly successful business leaders with dyslexia are Richard Branson, founder of Virgin Enterprises; investment banker Charles Schwab; and Paul Orfalea, founder of Kinko's.

Of course, some careers present greater barriers than others for a young person with dyslexia. One reason that so many individuals with dyslexia end up running their own businesses may be that they didn't do so well working for someone else; it helps to be in a managerial position where a secretary or administrative assistant can take care of typing, proofreading, and filing.

Generally, young people with dyslexia tend to do better with jobs that allow them to express creativity through their work, such as working as a graphic artist. This includes writing, such as television writer Stephen Cannell, or mystery writers Agatha Christie and Elizabeth Daniels Squire. Of course professional writers have editors available to proofread their work if they have continuing difficulty with the nuances of spelling and punctuation. Many youngsters do well with jobs involving sales, relying on their interpersonal skills.

The key to success is to mesh interests with natural abilities. If your teen plans to defer college, it may be helpful for him to work with a vocational or career counselor for ideas about where to start looking for work or training when he finishes high school. Many youngsters will find their own way, led by their own interests, with long-term employment evolving from a high school job or volunteer position.

Keep in mind that the transition from childhood to adult employment is difficult for many youngsters, and your child may explore many options before he finds his niche. Your child's imaginative approach and divergent learning style may lead him to take an unorthodox path, but as he moves into adulthood what he needs most from you is your faith, encouragement, and support. Recognize that success in many endeavors depends far more on social skills and personal qualities such as persistence and resilience than on the academic skills that were so important to school success. Your now-grown child will do best in areas that excite his passions. Encourage your child to follow his dreams—in the end, you may find yourself pleasantly surprised, or perhaps astounded, by how much your once-struggling child is able to accomplish in his adult life.

High Achievers with Dyslexia

Historical and Contemporary Figures

The following individuals had characteristics of thinking and learning that are commonly associated with dyslexia. Although we cannot know for certain if they had dyslexia, many had significant difficulties learning to read or other academic problems during childhood; yet they grew to be successful and influential adults. Here is what they said about their learning problems.

Leonardo da Vinci

Wrote his notes right to left, in mirror image; manuscripts contain many spelling errors characteristic of dyslexia.

> *"You should prefer a good scientist without literary abilities than a literate one without scientific skills."*

Andrew Jackson

Had difficulty writing; disliked reading. His spelling was so notoriously bad that it became an issue during his 1828 campaign for president.

"It's a damn poor mind that can only think of one way to spell a word."

Thomas Edison

Poor school performance, difficulty with mathematics, unable to focus, difficulty with words and speech.

"My teachers say I'm addled . . . my father thought I was stupid, and I almost decided I must be a dunce."

William Butler Yeats

Extreme difficulty learning to read as a child; lifelong difficulties with spelling.

"My father was an angry and impatient teacher and flung the reading book at my head."

Winston Churchill:

Did poorly in school; had a childhood stutter.

"I was, on the whole, considerably discouraged by my school days. It was not pleasant to feel oneself so completely outclassed and left behind at the beginning of the race."

Albert Einstein

Considered to be a slow learner as a child; denied admission to Swiss Federal Institute of Technology after failing entrance exams.

"One had to cram all this stuff into one's mind for the examinations, whether one liked it or not.

This coercion had such a deterring effect on me that, after I had passed the final examination, I found the consideration of any scientific problems distasteful to me for an entire year."

Pablo Picasso

Difficulty recognizing letters and numbers in childhood; unable to read until teenage years.

"Painting is just another way of keeping a diary."

Contemporary Figures

Here is what some contemporary figures have said about their dyslexia and learning problems:

George Burns, actor

"For me the toughest thing about dyslexia was learning to spell it."

Stephen J. Cannell, screenwriter and producer

"Since I was the stupidest kid in my class, it never occurred to me to try and be perfect, so I've always been happy as a writer just to entertain myself."

Cher, singer and actress

"I never read in school. I got really bad grades—Ds and Fs and Cs in some classes, and As and Bs in other classes. In the second week of the 11th grade, I just quit."

Agatha Christie, writer

"I, myself, was always recognized . . . as the 'slow one' in the family. It was quite true, and I knew it and accepted it. Writing and spelling were always terribly difficult for me. . . . I was . . . an extraordinarily bad speller and have remained so until this day."

Tom Cruise, actor

"I had to train myself to focus my attention. I became very visual and learned how to create mental images in order to comprehend what I read."

Danny Glover, actor

"Kids made fun of me because I was dark skinned, had a wide nose, and was dyslexic. Even as an actor, it took me a long time to realize why words and letters got jumbled in my mind and came out differently."

Dr. John R. Horner, paleontologist

"I barely made it through school. I read real slow. But I like to find things that nobody else has found, like a dinosaur egg that has an embryo inside. Well, there are 36 of them in the world, and I found 35."

Bruce Jenner, Olympic gold medalist

"I just barely got through school. The problem was a learning disability, at a time when there was nowhere to get help."

Magic Johnson, athlete

"The looks, the stares, the giggles . . . I wanted to show everybody that I could do better and also that I could read."

Keira Knightley, actress

"When I was very little, kids called me stupid because I couldn't read. . . . the dyslexia didn't help, but it's amazing what a child calling you stupid would do to make you read pretty quickly."

Keanu Reeves, actor

"Growing up, I had a lot of trouble reading, and so I wasn't a good student at all. Eventually I got fed up and I didn't bother to finish high school. I thought it was a waste of time—at least for me it was."

Nelson Rockefeller, governor of New York and U.S. vice president

"I was one of the 'puzzle children' myself—a dyslexic . . . And I still have a hard time reading today."

Nolan Ryan, athlete

"When I had dyslexia, they didn't diagnose it as that. It was frustrating and embarrassing. I could tell you a lot of horror stories about what you feel like on the inside."

Charles Schwab, investment banker

"I couldn't read. I just scraped by. My solution back then was to read classic comic books because I could figure them out from the context of the pictures. Now I listen to books on tape."

Jackie Stewart, international racecar driver

"For a dyslexic who does not yet know they are dyslexic, life is like a big high wall you never think you will be able to climb or get over. The moment you understand there is something called dyslexia, and there are ways of getting around the problem, the whole world opens up."

Victor Villasenor, author

"Once the fog lifts, dyslexics are prone to genius. Because theirs is such a unique way of looking at reality."

Helpful Internet Resources

General Information about Dyslexia, Literacy, and Learning

BrainConnection: The brain and learning
A web resource from Scientific Learning
www.brainconnection.com

Children of the Code
A public television DVD and web documentary series
www.childrenofthecode.org

Dyslexia Discovery Exhibit
A project of the Cookie Munchers Charitable Trust
www.cmct.org.nz/dde/

Dyslexia, the Gift
Information and resources for dyslexia
www.dyslexia.com

Dyslexia Talk: Dyslexia discussion board
www.dyslexiatalk.com

A Framework for Understanding Dyslexia
http://excellence.qia.org.uk/page.aspx?o=framework4dyslexia

The Florida Center for Reading Research
www.fcrr.org

International Dyslexia Association
Promoting literacy through research, education, and
advocacy
www.interdys.org

LDOnline
Learning disabilities information for parents, teachers, and
professionals
www.ldonline.org

Learning Disabilities Association of America
www.ldanatl.org

Reading Rockets: Launching young readers
www.readingrockets.org

What Works Clearinghouse
Institute of Education Sciences, U.S. Department of
Education
http://ies.ed.gov/ncee/wwc/

Programs and Therapies

**Academy of Orton-Gillingham Practitioners and
Educators**
www.ortonacademy.org

All Kinds of Minds
A nonprofit institute for the understanding of differences in
learning
www.allkindsofminds.org

Audiblox
A multisensory learning program
www.audiblox2000.com

Balametrics
Products for balance and sensory integration
www.balametrics.com

Berard Auditory Integration Training Services
www.auditoryintegration.net

Brain Gym International
www.braingym.org

BrainSkills
Online tools to build cognitive skills
www.brainskills.com

College of Optometrists in Vision Development
Vision therapy resources and referral list
www.covd.org

Davis Dyslexia Correction
Information and provider directory
www.dyslexiahelp.com

Earobics
Software to build phonemic awareness skills
www.earobics.com

Fast ForWord Learning Products
Software to build reading and phonemic awareness skills
www.scilearn.com

Great Leaps Reading
Building fluency, phonics, and motivation
www.greatleaps.com

Interactive Metronome
Advanced training for the brain
www.interactivemetronome.com

Internet Special Education Resources
Referral information for assessment, treatment, and advocacy
www.iser.com

Irlen Institute
Treatment for Scotopic Sensitivity Syndrome
www.irlen.com

Levinson Medical Center for Learning Disabilities
www.levinsonmedical.com

Lindamood-Bell Learning Systems
www.lindamoodbell.com

Masonic Learning Centers for Children
www.childrenslearningcenters.org

The RAVE-O Program
The Center for Reading and Language Research—Tufts University
http://ase.tufts.edu/crlr/raveo.html

Read America!
Phono-Graphix Reading Program
www.readamerica.net

Legal Resources and Information

Building the Legacy: IDEA 2004
U.S. Department of Education
http://idea.ed.gov

FairTest
The National Center for Fair and Open Testing
www.fairtest.org

Home School Legal Defense Association
www.hslda.org

National Disability Rights Network
Protection and Advocacy for Individuals with Disabilities
www.napas.org

Technical Assistance Alliance for Parent Centers
To help families of children and youth with disabilities
www.taalliance.org

Wrightslaw—Special Education law and advocacy
www.wrightslaw.com

Curriculum Materials and Support

AVKO Spelling Materials
www.spelling.org

Crossbow Education Dyslexic Teaching Resources
http://crossboweducation.com

Lexia Reading Software
www.lexialearning.com

Math-U-See
Manipulative materials for understanding math concepts
http://mathusee.com

Onion Mountain Technology
Low-tech tools for learning assistance
www.onionmountaintech.com

Recording for the Blind and Dyslexic
Educational Audiobooks for students with print and learning disabilities
www.rfbd.org

Resource Room
Tools, strategies, and structured explorations for interesting learners
www.resourceroom.net

RightStart Mathematics
Hands-on and visual system for learning math
www.alabacus.com

Rosetta Stone Language Learning Software
Interactive foreign language Instruction
www.rosettastone.com

SparkNotes
Study guides and literature
www.sparknotes.com

Total Physical Response
Foreign language instruction
www.tpr-world.com

Assistive Technology

AlphaSmart
Laptop computers for school use
www.alphasmart.com

Dyslexic.com
Technology for dyslexia
www.dyslexic.com

ReadingPen
The personal reading assistant
www.readingpen.com

ReadOn
Interactive software for people with reading difficulties
www.readonsoftware.com

Appendix C

Recommended Reading

General Reference and Information

Canter, Lee and Hausner Lee. *Homework Without Tears*. (Collins, 1993)

Cobb, Joyanne. *Learning How to Learn: Getting Into and Surviving College When You Have a Learning Disability*. (Child & Family Press, revised edition, 2003)

Cole, David, and Jonathan Mooney. *Learning Outside the Lines: Two Ivy League Students with Learning Disabilities and ADHD Give You the Tools For Academic Success and Educational Revolution*. (Fireside, 2000)

Fink, Rosalie. *Why Jane and John Couldn't Read—and How They Learned: A New Look at Striving Readers*. (International Reading Association, 2006)

Frank, Robert, and Kathryn E. Livingston. *The Secret Life of the Dyslexic Child: How She Thinks. How He Feels. How They Can Succeed*. (Rodale Press, 2004)

Hayden, Dierdre, Cheryl Takemoto, Winifred Anderson, and Stephen Chitwood. *Negotiating the Special Education*

Maze: A Guide for Parents and Teachers. (Woodbine House; 4th edition, 2008)

Kurnoff, Shirley. *The Human Side of Dyslexia: 142 Interviews with Real People Telling Real Stories about Their Coping Strategies with Dyslexia—Kindergarten through College.* (London Universal Publishing, 2001)

Levine, Mel. *The Myth of Laziness.* (Simon & Schuster, 2003)

———. *A Mind at a Time.* (Simon & Schuster, 2002)

Nosek, Kathleen. *The Dyslexic Scholar: Helping Your Child Succeed in the School System.* (Taylor Trade Publishing, 1995)

Palladino, Lucy Jo. *Dreamers, Discoverers and Dynamos: How to Help the Child Who Is Bright, Bored and Having Problems in School.* (Ballantine Books, 1999)

Shaywitz, Sally. *Overcoming Dyslexia: A New and Complete Science-Based Program for Reading Problems at Any Level.* (Knopf, 2003)

Siegel, Lawrence M., and Marcia Stewart. *The Complete IEP Guide: How to Advocate for Your Special Ed Child.* (Nolo Press, 5th edition, 2007)

Sousa, David A. *How the Brain Learns to Read.* (Corwin Press, 2004)

Stevens, Suzanne H. *The LD Child and ADHD Child: Ways Parents and Professionals Can Help.* (John F. Blair Publisher; revised subsequent edition, 1996)

Stowe, Cynthia M. *How To Reach and Teach Children and Teens with Dyslexia: A Parent and Teacher Guide to Helping Students of All Ages Academically, Socially, and Emotionally.* (Jossey-Bass, 2002)

Vitale, Barbara Meister. *Unicorns Are Real: A Right-Brained Approach to Learning.* (Grand Central Publishing, 1986)

West, Thomas G. *In the Mind's Eye: Visual Thinkers, Gifted People with Learning Difficulties, Computer Images, and the Ironies of Creativity.* (Prometheus Books; updated subsequent edition, 1997)

Winebrenner, Susan. *Teaching Kids with Learning Difficulties in the Regular Classroom.* (Free Spirit Publishing, revised updated edition, 2005)

Wolf, Maryanne. *Proust and the Squid: The Story and Science of the Reading Brain.* (Harper Perennial, reprint edition 2008)

Wright, Peter W.D., and Pamela Darr Wright. *From Emotions to Advocacy: The Special Education Survival Guide.* (Harbor House Law Press, 2006)

Specific Methods and Strategies for Dyslexia and Learning

Davis, Ronald D., and Eldon M. Braun. *The Gift of Dyslexia: Why Some of the Smartest People Can't Read . . . and How They Can Learn.* (Perigee Trade, subsequent edition 1997)

———. *The Gift of Learning: Proven New Methods for Correcting ADD, Math and Handwriting Problems.* (Perigee Trade, 2003)

Freed, Jeffrey, and Laurie Parsons. *Right-Brained Children in a Left-Brained World: Unlocking the Potential of Your ADD Child.* (Simon & Schuster, 1998)

Hannaford, Carla, and Candace Pert. *Smart Moves: Why Learning Is Not All in Your Head.* (Great River Books, 2nd revised expanded edition, 2005)

Irlen, Helen. *Reading by the Colors.* (Perigee Trade, updated edition, 2005)

Levinson, Harold N. *Smart but Feeling Dumb.* (Grand Central Publishing, revised updated subsequent edition, 2003)

McGuinness, Carmen, and Geoffrey McGuinness. *Reading Reflex: The Foolproof Phono-Graphix Method for Teaching Your Child to Read.* (Free Press, 1999)

Spalding, Romalda Bishop, and Mary Elizabeth North. *The Writing Road to Reading: The Spalding Method of Phonics for Teaching Speech, Writing and Reading.* (Collins, 5th revised edition, 2003)

Books for Children

Betancourt, Jeanne. *My Name Is Brain Brian.* (Scholastic Paperbacks 1995) [Ages 9–12]

Burton, Diane. *The Alphabet War: A Story about Dyslexia* (Albert Whitman & Company, 2004) [Ages 4–8]

Fisher, Gary L., Rhoda Cummings, and Jacki Urbanovic. *The Survival Guide for Kids with LD.* (Free Spirit Publishing, 2002) [Ages 9–12]

Gehret, Jeanne. *The Don't-Give-Up Kid and Learning Differences.* (Verbal Images Press, 1996) [Ages 9–12]

Gladden, Linda, and Ann Root. *Charlie's Challenge.* (Linda Gladdin 1995) [Ages 4–10]

Levinson, Harold N. *The Upside-Down Kids.* (M. Evans and Company, 1991) [Grades 3–8]

Polacco, Patricia. *Thank You, Mr. Falker.* (Philomel, 1998) [Ages 4–10]

INDEX

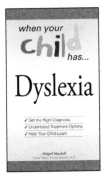